The Perfect Salesperson

RICK MANSFIELD

THE PERFECT SALESPERSON

Your Guide to Skilful Selling

2006

RICK MANSFIELD

THE PERFECT SALESPERSON
Your Guide to Skilful Selling

2006

The Perfect Salesperson

CONTENTS.

Rick Mansfield.

Rick Mansfield has been selling for over thirty years. He started as a lowly company representative and struggled to support a young family. Over the years he learned to listen to those people he felt were better at selling than him. He kept a journal. This was no ordinary diary. This journal was made up of all the ideas he gleaned from colleagues, managers, clients as well as speakers he listened to at seminars and sales meetings. His journal grew and as it did he put those ideas he felt worthwhile into practice. Soon he was topping the pole and outselling those around him.

One day he heard an idea that struck a chord and he told his company about it. They weren't interested!

What did he do? He took his idea, left the company and together with another salesman, Peter Bunney, started a business. At first it wasn't easy; houses had to be mortgaged and office premises arranged. There were many times when

Rick looked at the empty office and had to grit his teeth and hang on to his idea. Recruiting started and he determined to hire people who had never sold anything before. No inherited bad habits and no pre-conceived ideas!

Nine years later and with fourteen offices nationally, the company had over six hundred salespeople the bulk of which had never sold before.

Here was a multi-million dollar company built on an idea and experience, using information based on a journal that had been kept over the years.

Rick and Peter had become what the world calls successful businessmen.

Rick Mansfield.

Rick Mansfield has been selling for over thirty years. He started as a lowly company representative and struggled to support a young family. Over the years he learned to listen to those people he felt were better at selling than him. He kept a journal. This was no ordinary diary. This journal was made up of all the ideas he gleaned from colleagues, managers, clients as well as speakers he listened to at seminars and sales meetings. His journal grew and as it did he put those ideas he felt worthwhile into practice. Soon he was topping the pole and outselling those around him.

One day he heard an idea that struck a chord and he told his company about it. They weren't interested!

What did he do? He took his idea, left the company and together with another salesman, Peter Bunney, started a business. At first it wasn't easy; houses had to be mortgaged and office premises arranged. There were many times when

Rick looked at the empty office and had to grit his teeth and hang on to his idea. Recruiting started and he determined to hire people who had never sold anything before. No inherited bad habits and no pre-conceived ideas!

Nine years later and with fourteen offices nationally, the company had over six hundred salespeople the bulk of which had never sold before.

Here was a multi-million dollar company built on an idea and experience, using information based on a journal that had been kept over the years.

Rick and Peter had become what the world calls successful businessmen.

To The Three Lovely Ladies In My Life; My Wife Elaine And My Daughters, Lynn And Marina. Their Encouragement, Love And Constant Positive Outlook Have Always Sustained Me In Good And Not So Good Times. Thanks Girls!

INTRODUCTION.
(Effort and reward.)

For many years I worked as a commission salesman, earning my entire income from commissions I made on sales. Now this method of payment cuts both ways. On the plus side, the opportunity to earn a very high income is present but this goes hand in hand with the chance of earning little or nothing! You have to make sales to survive; no retainer; no salary; nothing to fall back on.

Some people enjoy the freedom this gives them and revel in the ability to earn in direct proportion to their ability and effort. Others can't take this kind of pressure and prefer to have a guaranteed income to rely on. Others take the middle road and work on a mixture of commission and salary. Different industries work in different ways. To put this another way; the higher the risk, the higher the income but, of course, the bigger the fall if things go wrong!

One day things went wrong for me, I suffered a burst appendix. Unfortunately it took the doctors two days to discover the cause of my pain and by then I had the whole bit, peritonitis, the lot!

Naturally it took me some weeks in hospital to recover, and with the help of antibiotics I got rid of the poisons that invaded my body. When I left hospital I weighed less than 112lbs and was still in need of rest and recuperation. However

I was a commission salesman and to my regret, had not had the foresight to effect income protection insurance.

I was responsible for my wife, two girls at school and a sizable mortgage.

I had to go out and earn some money!

It was at this point I decided to do something that I swore I would never do.

"If ever I have to go out and knock on doors, forget it, I'm leaving the selling business!"

But you know it's funny, when you have to go—you go.

It was the dead of winter. It was cold, windswept, wet and cheerless. It was a good time to be home in front of a cheerful fire. But I had a mortgage and bills and a family to support so really I had no choice! Luckily I had a nice warm overcoat to keep out the winter winds so off I went!

I drove to a housing estate nearby and climbed out of the car. The wind buffeted me as I walked up the first pathway to the first front door. I can still get a feel of what it was like, walking up that little path to knock on the door. Every nerve in my body was screaming out, *"This is not for you!"* and that was true. I had never seen myself as a doorknocker. That was for others to do. Not me! *I* was the consummate professional. I had been in the business of selling for over fifteen years and had dealt with senior executives and professionals about their money needs. My market was the 'upper socio-economic strata', yet here I was walking up to a stranger's front door, in the rain and in the cold winter's wind, I had just spent several weeks in hospital and needed a rest.

They say, "When the going gets tough the tough get going". I must say I didn't feel very tough, I felt cold and weak.

The first door opened to reveal a large housewife who was

obviously in the middle of preparing dinner for her family. She wore an apron and her hands were covered in flour. "Good evening" I said, "My name is Rick Mansfield of..."

"No thanks!" and the door slammed shut.

I stared at the number on the door and turning around walked down the path and along to the next little gate; I proceeded reluctantly up to the next front door. I would like to be able to say that the person behind the second door was more receptive but I can't. It was the same with the third, fourth and so on.

I had knocked on six doors and was feeling, as you can imagine, down about as far as I could go. As I approached the seventh door I made a decision that this would be the last. I didn't like what I was doing and although I had heard the expression, "Successful people do the things that failures don't like to do," I believed that this was above and beyond the call of duty!

I knocked on door number seven. It was opened by a man in his mid-fifties who smiled at me, listened to what I had to say and instead of refusing to talk, invited me in. He must have taken pity on me and as I stumbled in, he asked me if I would like a cup of tea. Oh, what a welcome that was! There are certain actions that restore one's faith in human nature and this was one of them.

We sat down in front of a warm open fire and I told him what I was about and what service I was offering. He listened intently to all I had to say and said, "I don't think you can be of any service to me." As I began to summon up some solid answers to objections, he said, "The people you need to speak to are young and have enough time to save." I had to agree. "I happen to be the headmaster of a boys boarding school here in town," he said, "and I have several young teachers who live in, aren't they the kind of people you need to talk to? Just a minute." He got up, went into the next room and returned straight away with a list of those teachers. Names, telephone numbers in their rooms and a roster of when they would be working and when they were free and said, "Here you are, *tell them I sent you!*" This was manna from heaven! I could not have expected a better result. I was warm. I was drinking a friendly cup of tea, and I had just been given several of the best referred-leads anywhere! These were leads from the boss, *"Tell them I sent you!"* The phrase kept ringing in my ears.

Over the next few weeks I managed to sell each of those teachers and in addition some of their friends as well. I was back in business!

Make no mistake I was nearly out. Nearly done for! The reason I have gone to the trouble to tell you this story, is that I believe that *every* time you put in an effort you *get a result!*

It may not happen straight away, but you will and must get a result of some kind. So it stands to reason that it is *always worth putting in the effort!* Effort is never wasted. Let me explain. This little door knocking exercise kept me in the business. I went on to take over the area management for the company and built a very successful branch for them.

Some years later I met a man who was to become my business partner, Peter Bunney. Peter and I together, built a large company selling financial services. We trained and controlled over six hundred sales personnel writing more business than any other group in the country. This agency was eventually sold to a large financial institution for a multi-million dollar sum and we became what the world calls 'successful businessmen'.

What have these seven doors got to do with all of this?

I sometimes think back to that cold bleak evening and think of those seven doors, and I have tried to calculate what each one was worth to my family and me. How much money was I actually earning as I walked up those unfriendly paths? It's hard to come to an exact figure, but each one must be worth several hundred thousand dollars. Had I known *that* at the time it would have made that unpleasant task a little easier to bear.

Do you get paid for your activity in business? Yes, you sure do! You get paid for it—*always!* I believe that an understanding of this simple philosophy is so important because it creates all the difference between the mediocre and the brilliant. Those who understand will never again say, "It's no good doing that, it doesn't work" or "Don't waste your time talking to this group or that person, they have been approached before and said, 'No!'"

By taking action you will and must be paid at some time. Even if all you gain is a little more experience, you will and must have made a profit. Sit still, do nothing and you will lose.

So keep records. Records of your phone calls—successful and unsuccessful, your appointments, your interviews, your closing interviews, your sales, your earnings, the size of your sales, times and so on. The more you know about your activity the richer you can become and the more confidence you will have. You will know with absolute certainty that if you do this and this and this you will succeed! It is as certain as any other proven scientific equation.

Effort is always rewarded!

1.
Selling, what is it?

Perhaps it would be a good idea to start this book on professional persuasion by trying to find out what it is. What do we mean by the phrase "He sold me this" or "I sold them the idea"?

It seems clear that people who have been sold something have taken an action that maybe they would not normally take. Have they been motivated by some *outside* influence to buy?

It is this idea of an outside persuasive force that I believe causes misunderstanding of salespeople and the sales process. Some people believe that salespeople can make them do things against their will. I believe this is rarely the case. If it did happen then it isn't a sale; it won't stick. In fact it does the salesperson more harm than good. Why? Because the customer isn't happy and unhappy customers create failed businesses.

When we take a buying decision it is rarely done because of the strong influence of an outside force. If that were true we would always be bending to the will of others. Being obedient to them. Following orders. This kind of motivation works of necessity in the armed forces where people have to follow orders in situations of life and death; situations where actions must occur, that the individual would not normally contemplate. Nobody "sells" the idea of the soldier "going over the top". He does so because he has been conditioned by rigorous training.

This training *is* persuasion certainly, but it is not selling, *it is compelling—ordering—telling.*

And telling isn't selling!

Something very different happens in the sales process and the purpose of this book is to discover what this process is and how we can utilise it to improve our sales ability for the good of, not only ourselves, but of the consumer.

We must, as salespeople, achieve a basic understanding of what *motivates* people. What turns us on and gets us going?

What happens inside our thought processes that causes us to take action or not, to walk or run, to talk or listen, to run or fight, *to buy or reject?*

Before any salesperson can truly understand what selling is all about, he or she must first realise that **people do things for their own reasons—not ours.**

Unless there is some kind of mental or physical coercion involved, then the things we do, we do for our own satisfaction and well being. Even those people who work for the downtrodden all over the world and appear to be truly selfless, are taking actions that give them satisfaction and fulfilment, they wouldn't have it any other way. This in no way denigrates their actions. It *validates* them. If we had all been running around doing things that gave us no satisfaction, no pleasure, no gain of any kind, then the human race would not have survived. It *has* survived, and more than that, it has *achieved.* We have reached out and done things that are almost incomprehensible.

This idea that 'people do things for their own reasons, not ours', must be at the basis of all our actions in selling if we are to succeed. When we forget and try to make somebody do something for *our* reasons, we fail to achieve what we want—a sale!

We sometimes hear the phrase 'high pressure salesman' and I must say at the outset I have never understood what 'high pressure selling' means. It seems to me to be a contradiction in terms because it implies some kind of outside pressure that would cause the buyer to take some action that is bad for him. Outside pressure and doing harm has no place in the selling process. It achieves nothing for either party and always does more harm than good!

The only sale that is worthwhile is one that benefits both buyer and seller! The seller benefits by the profitable conclusion to the sale and the buyer benefits because he has done something for his or her reasons. Two winners! *This 'win-win' situation is really the only proper end result of our activities as salespeople.* Of the many salespeople I have recruited and trained over the last thirty years, it has been those people who genuinely *care about the other person's welfare,* who create long-term careers.

The salesperson who can go about his or her business, being of value to clients and prospective clients, always being able to see things from the *other person's* viewpoint and understand that it is the *other person's reasons* that will create a positive decision, will win in this very competitive profession. A top salesperson finds out what the consumer wants and then helps him get it.

In saying this I wouldn't want you to run away with the idea that we must give in to all the comments made by the prospect. To agree with every statement made in the mistaken belief that this will in some way get the prospect on our side, will only lead to weak selling and poor results. There is a marked difference between sympathy and empathy, and you will learn what this is, as you learn the techniques you need to become a professional persuader.

Nothing happens until the salesperson sells something.

Once the researchers and the inventors, the scientists and the dreamers have done their work and created a product or service, it must be sold. That is the way commerce works. All products and services must be sold to prospects—and at a profit. If the salespeople of the world aren't out there getting 'yes's', then it's all for nothing.

This surely means that we salespeople are important to the economy; you could almost say we *are* the economy! We are the movers and shakers. You might have the best mouse trap ever designed, the best airliner in the world, the greatest service ever devised for the good of mankind, but if it is never sold, then it doesn't really exist does it? *It is all for nothing!*

If you are in selling now or thinking about taking it up as a career, then you must realize the enormous responsibility and opportunity that lies before you.

Selling can take you to the very pinnacle of the particular mountain you want to climb. It can give you all the job satisfaction, not to mention material satisfaction, the world can offer. You will be one of those unique people who is always in demand, never idle, respected by clients and industry alike as a valuable and indispensable member of the commercial world.

I hope as you read, you will be able to gain an understanding of selling and salesmanship and achieve the joy and satisfaction it has given me in the thirty plus years I have been privileged to be a salesman.

Many people ask what kind of selling they should aspire to? There seem to be so many different kinds of selling, ranging from shop sales staff, telephone salespeople, car salesmen, computer sales, life insurance, company reps. and so on.

Salespeople get paid in many different ways. Salary—salary plus commission—retainer plus commission—straight commission and more. Some are self employed, some employed and some hire out to different companies to achieve their aims.

If you are new to selling, you must talk to a lot of people in the business, ask a lot of questions, and make a firm decision. And once that decision is made go as hard as you can to get what you want.

There is one common distinguishing feature among all top salespeople—*they are all great askers!*

If you want something you must *ask for it,* and in the asking *expect to win.* Never be apologetic about asking for the things you want. Be prepared to defend your position and give good reasons for stating your requirements.

In the many interviews with aspiring salespeople that I have conducted it is the determined, positive person who wins with me, the person who is clearly excited by an opportunity, and although lacking experience comes through as keen, ambitious and energetic.

This person continually asks for what he wants. What do *you* want? Define it! Write it down. Be precise. Be clear *and above all be positive!*

Managers and sales managers are always looking for good people and trying to ascertain whether the person sitting in front of them has got the kind of positive qualities a good salesperson must have to succeed and sell the product.

Make no mistake a good salesperson is always in demand, in good times and bad, because companies always need to sell whatever it is they are offering. You must never doubt this. Self-doubt is one of the most destructive forces that can work its way into your brain and affect your attitude.

Some people say that many salespeople are over optimistic to the point of being unrealistic. To these people I can only say this,

'You can't be too optimistic!'

Many years ago I watched a flickering, black and white television on which an American President was saying that by the end of the decade an American would walk on the surface of the moon and return to Earth safely to tell us all about it. That kind of optimism is hard to believe. This was something no one had ever done!

A few short years later on another black and white screen, I saw a man in a space suit bounce down the ladder on to the moon's surface. *The moon's surface!*

That night my wife Elaine and I went out into the garden and looked up at the moon. This silent, cold, beautiful and mysterious body shining in the dark night sky and still we couldn't believe what we had seen on our TV screens only hours before. We tried to make out the Sea of Tranquillity where these men were and we were overawed. Optimism? Yes of course! It is what has made us great. Good salespeople *are* optimistic, for them *there are no limits—only horizons!* If you can dream and think big and be what we call a 'blue-skies' person, then seriously consider selling as a career. We need you!

As you go through the chapters of this book take the time to make notes. Think about what you have read and imagine yourself in real life situations.

It may be that the prospect has not quite got the message you are trying to get across. What is a better way of communicating this information? Watch for signs of interest or disinterest. Are you getting through?

One great phrase to remember is *'telling isn't selling'*, so many salespeople think by telling, they are getting through. It ain't necessarily so!

There are much better ways than telling and these will unfold in the following pages. There are better ways than 'talking the hind leg off a donkey'. There are better ways than hiding the truth or worse still telling lies. Good salespeople don't need to 'gild the lily'. If your product is good it will stand on it's own merits and if it's no good you shouldn't be selling it. You have to live with your actions in selling for a long time.

Many salespeople fear rejection more than they should. We have a section in this book to help you overcome this irrational fear. Rejection is inevitable and those of us who sell for a living could not continue if rejection knocked us about too much.

Of course nobody likes a 'no', we would much rather get a 'yes'. It is in our understanding of the *process* of selling that the professional sails through the 'no's' with pleasure, knowing that the 'no' will always be there to *help* him on his way.

Let's get out there and see how many 'no's' we can get on any given day. I'll make a bet with you. *If you can get more 'no's' than the next person then you will get more 'yes's'.* That means you will earn more money than the next person, build a better future and achieve higher goals.

'No's' are a part of selling, not an impediment. Without them we can't succeed!

In a world where the 'no' doesn't exist you will find no salespeople.

We are not required in a land where everyone agrees to buy; where everyone says 'yes'. The sale actually begins when the prospect says 'no'. It is in the ability to convert a 'no' into a 'yes' that we achieve the heights.

The tougher it is out there the more the salesperson shines, because it is under these conditions that the 'pro' flourishes. It is when the pressure is on, the resistance is strong and the objections are voiced that we, the closers of the world come to the fore.

I remember hearing a sales manager saying once "Tom would be a good salesman if only he could close!" What nonsense! If Tom can't close he is nowhere near being any kind of salesman. Presenter? Maybe. Educator? Perhaps. Motivator? Could be. Salesperson? No! *He can't close!*

Salespeople are closers of sales and closers of sales get people to take action. They make things happen. They move goods and services.

A Lawyer is no lawyer if he can't win cases. A doctor is no doctor if he can't diagnose and prescribe. A pilot is no pilot if he can't land a plane *and a salesperson is no salesperson if he or she can't close sales*!

To whom do we sell? Where do we find the people who could buy our products or services and how do we get in touch with them?

This subject of prospecting is so often missed by sales trainers and yet without people to talk to we are lost—nowhere to go and no reason for going. How much better would any salesperson be if he or she learned how to prospect.

There are people and organisations everywhere who need what we have to offer, so we must find ways of getting in front of these potential customers. Prospecting is therefore another major topic in the art of selling and many and varied are the ways.

'If you give a man a fish he will eat for a day. Teach him how to fish and he will eat for a lifetime!'

I hope to be able to teach you how to fish, because this knowledge will make you indispensable to any employer and increase your earnings many fold. You will write your own ticket. Nobody will ever be able to make *you* redundant because you are a professional prospector. How then, do you get your message across to your prospect? Do you play it by ear? Ad-lib it? Wing it? Oh I hope not! The Professional Persuader goes into any selling situation fully prepared to tell his story and show his wares with a properly constructed well-prepared and rehearsed presentation.

A presentation that has been carefully worked out to achieve all the right responses, to unfold in a logical and yet motivating sequence, all the information the prospect needs to make a sound decision. 'Ad-libbing' is simply not good enough. You wouldn't expect an actor to ad-lib his way through Hamlet would you? No, of course not. The master words must be just right!

We will discuss presenting your case in such a way that, if a sale is to be made, you are the one who is going to make it!

There are four major activities that we must all do *very well* if we are to succeed.

The four 'Pillars of Success in Selling' are as follows:—

1. **Prospecting.**
2. **Appointing.**
3. **Presenting.**

4. Closing.

Soon you will be well on your way to mastering the four pillars of success in selling! .

2.
Prospecting: The Essential Ingredient.

Some years ago I was sitting in the waiting room of a large accountancy firm reading the out of date magazines, when a young man came in with a bundle of papers under his arm, he took a sheaf of these papers and handed them to the receptionist saying he was from one of the large mutual life insurance companies and here was their new calendar.

He explained that he was the local representative, which surprised me as he looked rather down at heel. This young man, who I am sure called himself a salesman, then turned round and walked out the door, and as I watched, the receptionist picked up the new calendar resplendent with the company logo, glanced at it, and threw it in the waste paper basket!

For a large *(and I mean large!)* financial institution to allow its image to be manhandled in this way, there has to be something seriously wrong with their marketing and sales training and the techniques they use.

The problem is that most members of the public think of salesmen (when they think of them) as being just like that young man. This happened many years ago and I had just become a salesman. I determined there and then never to allow myself to behave in such a useless manner and to always do my best to make every call a winner! To achieve some positive result, if only in a small way, from every contact I made. That is what salespeople do, don't they? They make contact; offer their service; approach people with a view to making a sale.

One thing I did know was that if I made *more calls* than other people, I would make *more money* than other people. But if I walked around delivering calendars I'd go broke. A sales career has got to be more rewarding and certainly more fulfilling than that! You could pay someone peanuts to deliver things.

One of the questions I'm most commonly asked by people thinking of entering a sales career is "whom do I sell to?" or "where do I find my prospects?" and it's a fair question. Without prospects we are out of business.

I like to start the answer to this question by establishing that prospects are in fact people. People just like you and me. These people all have various wants; desires, needs and wishes, just like us. There is one certain thing that we do know about people, and that is there are millions of them. We will never run of out people to see. In fact you could never see all the people who are prospects for whatever it is you are selling, even if you live ten life times. So can we agree then that there is no shortage of your most valuable resource, prospects?

How is it then that some salespeople always have plenty of people to offer their services to, and some are always struggling?

The answer lies in the fact that the successful salesperson has a *prospecting plan.* Not only does he have a plan, he makes sure he follows his or her plan without fail. I have no way of knowing what it is you sell or want to sell, but I do know this for sure, without a constant supply of good prospects all your good intentions will be grounded. Firstly, how can we define this activity we call prospecting?

I like to put it this way *prospecting in selling, is that activity which gets us in front of enough prospects, in a selling situation, to ensure that we achieve our own worthwhile goals.*

Prospecting is therefore at the very heart of our success. I would rather be a top prospector than a top presenter for instance, although I hope I'm good at both.

Top prospectors always have their antenna out and tuned no matter where they are. They look at everyone they meet as a prospect.

They understand that prospecting is a process, not a problem. It is, to use a cliché, *a numbers game*. The more you get the more you sell.

How can you plan your prospecting?

Before you can plan anything you must have a fundamental understanding of your business. You have to know certain facts about your industry and yourself.

Lets assume that to be really successful in your sales career you had to make five sales a week and that by keeping careful records you discovered, over a period of time, that to make one sale you had to have four presentations (we will explain these unfamiliar terms as we go along) and to have four presentations you had to make eight appointments. To make eight appointments you made twenty phone calls, and had to have twenty-five prospects to do that.

So one sale (a days work) needs twenty-five prospects, five days a week 25 x 5 =125 prospects each week to be really successful.

25 Prospects = 20 phone calls = 8 appointments = 4 presentations = 1 sale.

Naturally these figures may not apply to your industry so you have to *keep your own records and break them down in exactly the same way as I have done here.*

With all the facts at your fingertips you are now in a position to create a plan. A master-prospecting plan that will guarantee you will achieve your goals. No matter what they are. The beautiful thing about being a salesperson is you are master of your own destiny. You take charge of your own life. How many of us would like to do just that? What we make, we make, and we make it because *we have planned our activity,* for that is what we get paid for, *our activity.* Not what we *say* we are going to do, but what we *actually* do, on a planned day-to-day basis.

Before we rush out to gather all these wonderful prospects, wouldn't it be a good idea to find out what a prospect is for our particular business or industry? You can't sell pregnancy clothes to elderly ladies or Harley Davidson motorcycles to 10-year-old children, and it is pretty difficult to sell ice to Eskimos, no matter how good a salesperson you are. Each of us has to define our market and focus on that particular segment of the population.

If you were selling life insurance as an example you would want to talk to people who need, can afford and are healthy enough, to buy a life policy. Young married couples would be a good example, particularly if they were planning or had already started a family.

Research your particular industry and it's products, so you will know areas in which you should be prospecting.

If your product were to do with education, you would know whom to approach, or if it involved computers you would need to talk to people who use computers or who *could* use them. This field of computers is such a wide one that I am sure many salespeople specialise in one of it's many and varied applications.

Knowing who your prospects are doesn't get you in front of them. To get into a selling situation takes a little more than just knowing where they are or who they are. We have to achieve something that we don't normally have with these people. We have to achieve *approachability*. This is the key to long-term success in the prospecting field. Without *approachability* you will always be a stranger, a voice in the dark, just another salesperson.

I don't like beating my head against a brick wall—it hurts! So when I finally approach somebody, I like him or her to at least have heard of me, or to know somebody I know; I must have some kind of contact.

Approachability is vital in prospecting.

It can make all the difference to your daily activity. Let's work hard then, on ways of getting this approachability.

The number one, absolute best way of getting approachability is by using a referred lead. This comes from someone, perhaps a client, who has referred you on to somebody he or she knows and has not objected to the use of his or her name as a means of introduction.

You can imagine the phone call can't you "Mr. Brown?" "Yes" "My name is…. has John Smith mentioned my name to you recently?" Bingo! You are no longer a total stranger. You know his friend John. A referred lead has the strongest approachability of all prospects apart from your own clients and people you already know. They can make all the difference in your selling career.

You may be asking 'where do I get these referred leads?' Surely not everyone will offer to introduce me to those people he or she knows? My reply would be, *you won't get any if you don't ask. Good salespeople are good askers.* You must learn to ask all the time and from all the people.

Each of us is surrounded by a very familiar group of people. Our relations, our workmates, our fellow club or church members, people we play sport with and our close friends. The person you are asking has this circle and any one or all of these people could be prospects for you. You must learn to ask, and you must learn *how* to ask.

There are salespeople all over the world asking for referred leads and most of them are asking the wrong question.

What is the wrong question?

It goes like this; "Who do you know who would be interested in (your product or service)".

The nominator now scratches his head and tries to think and think and comes up with no one.

"I don't know!" he says, and the salesperson receives another knock-back to add to his collection for the day.

It is just like asking someone to give you names of people who want to learn French. "What!" I hear you say, "Learn French, how do I know?" Of course, how do you know? You are not telepathic. Unless they have told you they want to learn French, you wouldn't know would you? It is just as silly to ask, "Who do you know who would be interested in..." (your product or service?) Get the point?

It's the wrong question. Surely all you need to know from the nominator is *'who do you know?'* then it is up to you to qualify these people later. By 'qualify' I mean they will have a chance of wanting or needing your service. There is really only one way to find *that* out isn't there?

So the task of getting referred leads is to put specific people in the mind of the nominator so that he or she can tell you their names. "Who is your next door neighbour?" "If you were going to have a party on Saturday who would be the first four people you would invite?"

Specific people!

Are these the only prospects that you have got? No, of course not. As we said, the world is full of people. These people may want or need your service. All we need is a little bit of approachability.

What about warming the prospect up a bit by sending out a lead letter with just enough information to create interest and some advance warning that you will be contacting them on such and such a day. This method can be applied to lists as well as prospects you have noticed during your day's activity.

A word of caution here! Don't send out too many at one time. There is only one of you, and you can't follow up too many. Perhaps ten or fifteen per day with a definite plan of ring them in three days time. Make it a habit. Keep yourself active!

What about situation prospecting? You are in a particular situation, talking to a particular person, should you offer your service? Of course, you are a salesperson, and that is what salespeople do. They ask and they ask and they ask again!

You may be discussing a tradesman's quotation, visiting your accountant, buying some clothes or talking to your children's teacher. Ask! You have nothing to lose, everything to gain. It's what we salespeople do!

You can't expect anybody to buy from you, if they are not aware that you are selling.

What about the people *you* know?

Sometimes I hear the excuse, "Oh I don't want to impose on my friends." "I don't want to use the people I know." Let me assure you I can really understand that attitude. I used to say the same thing. Then one day a good friend took me aside. He was, and is, a salesman, and said, "Rick, what do you really think of this product you are trying to sell?" "I think it's wonderful!" I said. "Then why are you denying it to the people who are closest to you? Don't they deserve to see it first? Of course if you are ashamed of it, or there is something wrong with it, you would want to hide it away and only sell it to strangers wouldn't you?" *I saw the light!*

I began to understand that being a salesperson meant having the opportunity to help people, to show them something that they would value and want. If I didn't show it to them or at least give them opportunity to evaluate it for themselves then they might think there was something wrong with the product, and if there was something wrong with the product, then there must be something wrong with me. Why would I be selling a bad product otherwise?

There and then I determined to show my product every chance I had *and let the prospects decide whether it was for them or not!*

It's all part of prospecting.

Never pre-judge! The most unlikely people buy, as do the most likely! Don't forget people do things for their reasons, not ours, and we can't find out their reasons if we don't ask. The worst they can say to you is "no thanks." Nothing lost, no egos damaged, no friendships destroyed! The more we ask the more we get. The future for the asker is always better than the timid non-asker. The person who pre-judges a situation and fails to act can't achieve. You can't pre-judge any situation. It is in the future and the future is given to no one. It will unfold in its own time and all we can do is use that time in profit making activity.

Prospecting is a process and it's a process that we control by taking all the positive and productive actions we can.

Become a professional prospector. Keep you antenna out and tuned. You never know when someone will say to you "Yes, I think that's a great idea, sign me up!"

That's another sale, another client, and another brick in the wall of your future mansion.

Approachability by itself doesn't necessarily mean a person is a good prospect. There have to be some other qualities and of course there are. Before a person can become a prospect he or she has to be able to afford whatever it is you are offering. There is no much point in trying to sell to someone who has no money. How can we tell whether the prospect has money or not? Simply by asking the nominator about this person. Where do they work? What do they do there? Is this person married or single? Drive a car? Own a house! You may or may not need all this information in your business but it is for sure you will need some details about the prospect. What about need? Surely a prospect would have to need what you are going to offer? Well not necessarily. Many people don't buy simply because they need something.

Most people buy because they want something!

If need and want can go together so much the better. But how many times have we bought something we didn't really need simply because we wanted it?

For instance nobody *needs* a luxury car but plenty of people *want* one and are prepared to sacrifice large amounts of money to buy what they want. If you can make someone want something you are on the way to making a sale. So a prospect must have a need / want to qualify. What then, have we got so far?

A prospect is a person who has:—
1. Approachability.
2. Money.
3. Need / want for you product or service.

If you can discover some of this information before approaching anyone then you have done your homework and the prospect is qualified. You and they are something more than strangers and prospecting becomes simpler and above all *fun!*

This chapter wouldn't be complete if we didn't look at all the methods of prospecting. You may find one or more to be ideally suited to your business or your particular method of operation. These methods are in no special order as everyone's business is different. My suggestion is try them all and see what works. The great thing about selling is that you are able to experiment. Try new things and even invent a method and system all your own. You are always free to expand your thinking thereby expanding your horizons.

Methods:—

1. Cold Canvas. Sound dreadful? To some it is, and yet many successful and professional salespeople use it, and with great success. Going where the people are. It gets you in front of the most people in the shortest possible time. You may have to see more people per appointment but then as we said! There is no shortage of people!

Some salespeople swear they will never cold call. It's beneath them. To them I say. "Never forget you are a salesperson and it is your job to offer your service to as many people as you can in the time you have. That's what we salespeople do." Cold calling is usually door-to-door or business-to-business and can be used anytime to fill in the gaps, day or evening. A good approach is vital in this activity and we will learn all about this soon.

2. Cold Telephoning. This method is very similar to No.1 except that we don't go out and face the people. We use the quicker (and probably cheaper) method, of using the telephone. Aiming at a particular market may be important when telephoning so that at least you have a chance of talking to the right person.

Using the telephone as a means of getting in front of people will be discussed in detail later.

3. Direct mail. This is a method of 'warming up' a prospect—giving a little more of that all-important approachability. The secret is not to send out too many at once and follow each one up by either a face-to-face call or on the telephone. Lead-letters are no good if you don't follow up.

4. Advertising. 'Horses for courses' applies here. Some businesses rely very heavily on advertising to bring people to their door as well as coupon responses. One encyclopaedia firm that I know enjoys great success with coupon advertising followed up by a face-to-face call by the salesperson.

5. Clients. Oh dear, oh dear! What a neglected opportunity, our own clients, people who have bought from us. Does their situation change? Yes. Do they want and need other products and services? Yes. Then why on earth should we let someone else reap the benefits? Never forget your own clients.

6. Bird-dogs. People who are your eyes and ears; in the car trade they are called spotters. You can't be everywhere at once so other people who understand your business can help you to find out about and meet more prospects. If you can come to some financial arrangement with these 'bird-dogs' all the better, you are building a business and they can help.

7. Telemarketing. This is a method of paying someone else to telephone for appointments on your behalf. It doesn't suit all industries but it has one great advantage. It keeps you out in front of people selling, which is where you should be.

8. Sponsorships. When used correctly this can be an excellent method of prospecting. Make sure that your sponsorship is not just a monetary donation, but also a personal presence within the club or organisation. Find ways where you can contribute during the year in ways other than money. Perhaps by helping out at functions etc. and be present to give trophies you have sponsored. Make sure people know you are a sponsor.

9. Situation prospecting. A greatly misunderstood method covering a wide range of activity put simply it means whenever you are in a situation that enables you to offer your service—do it. You may have bought something, you may have sold something, you may be at a party or you may be playing a game of golf. In short any situation that brings you into contact with other people can and should be used as an opportunities to either prospect, appoint or sell. It is a big world out there and for you to make your mark in it, you have to make your presence felt!

10. Centres of influence. These are normally people who are in a position of authority or respect. They also know and respect you and are willing to refer you to other people because they know your service will be good and what you have will benefit those they refer to you. The salesperson that has a number of centres of influence is never short of good prospects.

Successful prospecting is the ingredient that changes a salesperson's life more than any other factor.

- You may have the greatest product or service ever created.
- You may have the most beautiful presentation ever devised.
- You may have the most effective closing techniques in the world.
- You may have the strongest desire to succeed coupled with the kind of dynamic energy that creates millionaires.

Yet even with all this going for you, *if you can't get in front of enough quality prospects then it's all academic!*

Salespeople need to see people—and plenty of them—and it is in the seeing of enough people that the problem is cured.

Imagine if I sat you down in an office and brought in real live prospects on a regular basis to be sold on the idea of your product or service. It would be a great job wouldn't it? All you would have to do is sit there and sell, sell, sell. You would be wealthy in no time at all because of all the sales you would make and the money you would earn.

But would you really be earning that money? What about the effort *I* would have to go to so that I could keep feeding you with people? Surely *I would be the one actually earning the money,* because it would be me that had to go out and find these people for you. It would be me paying for things like advertising, so that people came to your door. Without my efforts you would be very lonely and very poorly paid. People who work behind counters in stores don't get very well paid and yet they have to sell. I happen to believe that they should be paid much more for the job that they do. Particularly if they do it well. They are, or should be, the company's front line.

The problem is that once the advertising has been paid, once the rent has been met, once the stock has been bought, once the displays have been set up, once the light bill and the heating bill and the rates have been fixed, there isn't a lot left for the salesperson behind the counter.

Many costs have to be met to bring people into the store.

All the prospecting has been done and the salesperson merely shows up and sometimes sells the item, in most cases to a willing prospect. We get paid for value and *the valuable activity is prospecting.*

If you can get into a situation where prospecting is an important part of your activity, you will be well paid. Prospecting is therefore not a problem at all; *it is a well paid process!* It is a process that can be *learned* and activated by anyone with the desire to achieve high goals.

It takes a professional salesperson to *build a market so that their market will build them.*

It has been truly said, *"you must be careful who you call a salesperson—lest you flatter him!"*

Without a constant supply of quality prospects the salesperson will forever be struggling, reaching for the stars and never getting there!

With a constant supply of quality prospects the same person is transformed into a successful businessperson, always having someone new to approach and dealing on a warm and friendly basis. You can build a network of people who know and trust you and believe in your product or service.

Why is it do you think that relativity few salespeople are successful at prospecting? Is it that difficult? No not at all. Now don't get me wrong. I'm not saying it's easy. What we must do is *operate to a plan.*

I'm a great believer in living in the present; making each day, when it becomes today, worthwhile. Doesn't this mean that we should do everyday, those things that must be done? And then if we string these days together, end-to-end as it were, then we succeed. *A successful life is merely a series of successful days, one after the other.*

What would a successful day be for you in your business?

If we are talking prospecting and we are, you would need to know how many prospects you need to achieve your goals and the only way you can do that is to keep records of your actual activity, you must know what each part of your activity is worth, and the only way to find this out is to write it all down and analyse it. Right?

Perhaps it would help if I gave you a real life example.

Assume a sale is worth $800 to the salesperson. By keeping proper records over three months we discover that three full presentations (that is a presentation in which the prospect is asked to buy, or in other words the salesperson attempts to close)—results in one sale. But to get to those three presentations we have had to make ten appointments (Some say 'yes' some say 'no') and to achieve those ten appointments we needed twenty referred leads.

So the formula is as follows:—
Qualified prospects 20
Appointments made 10
Closing Presentations 3
Sales 1
Earnings $800

Now suppose your income goal is $1,600 per week. You know that over a reasonable period of time (in this case three months) $1600 requires forty prospects and if we take a five day working week, we need, on a daily basis a fifth of forty prospects—eight.

So now we know we have to get eight qualified prospects each day.

That means today!

When you wake up in the morning you know that if you are to achieve your goal you are going to have to get, from somewhere, eight qualified prospects. Let us suppose that for the sake of this exercise we mean referred leads. (I am going to show you how too get referred leads in a minute.)

We are going to have to make twenty appointments this week. That means four today. These appointments may be for tomorrow or next week or a month away but we must *make* four today.

This then, is a simple and workable plan; a plan that anyone can achieve. Bearing in mind that anyone *can,* not everyone *will.*

If you are determined to get four appointments today, then you know *over a period of time you will earn $1600 per week.*

You want to double this? Then double the number of appointments. Not enough time? Then increase the time. There is no law that says you can't sell on Saturday. The trouble with many salespeople is that they cram one week's work into four weeks instead of the other way around!

You are in charge. *You fill up your own 'in tray.'*

Now I'm going to give you a simple technique to get referred leads. If your business would benefit from referred lead prospecting, this is how to do it.

"John, I'm delighted that you have taken advantage of this (product / service) and become my client. As you know, my business is meeting people and showing them this idea. Of course I can only do this with your help.

Will you help me?"

Answer "Yes."

"Fine, of the people you know—family, friends, neighbours and so on, who can you think of who is doing well in business?"

As you say this write down one side of a blank piece of paper 1 to 10 and as soon as you get your first name write it down next to No.1 and say, *"Great. That's one—Fine. That's two..."* and so on until you achieve ten referred leads. Then go back and qualify these names by asking for all the information you need for your particular industry.

If the client queries whether you wish to use his name (no one wants their name to be 'used') say, *"Of course not John, I would never use your name in that way—**but may I say that know you?"***

This rarely fails.

or

"John, if (Jim) came in here right now you would introduce us wouldn't you?"

"Yes of course!"

"And that is the only way I would ever mention that I know you; merely as a means of introduction. Is that fair enough?"

Try it; it works!

If John has not bought from you, no problem, just change the first sentence—

"John, I'm delighted you have taken the time to look at this (product/idea/service) and even though it is not for you at the moment, perhaps it will be at sometime in the future."

Then carry on as before.

There are only a certain number of reasons that salespeople don't get enough referred leads.

1.   We don't ask.
2.   We procrastinate.
3.   We lack confidence.
4.   We lack technique.
5.   We fear rejection.

The cure is very simple, ***ask for leads!***

Some people think that they will upset the sale by asking and yet no sale was ever lost purely because the salesperson asked for a referral!

In fact, in many cases, the reverse is true. If what you are offering is valuable, wouldn't your new client be thinking of others it may benefit?

When should you ask?

a)   When you have completed a sale.
b)   When you have presented and received a 'no.'

c) At any service call on a client.

d) Whenever you have the opportunity.

You must ask and ask and ask; and always with *confidence*. Ask as though you *expect* referrals. That it is a normal part of your business practice.

How do you get yourself to do what has to be done?

The answer is simple daily goals. No formula will rocket you faster to financial independence than this one. Make this commitment, *'I will get 'x' number of referred leads everyday'* and you will ensure you always have somewhere to go and you will create that ingredient common to all top salespeople— *momentum!*

This is the start of a workable prospecting plan for you!

3.
Planning to succeed.

They say the job's not finished until the planning is done. And it's not started either! Planning is one of the biggest reasons for success in selling. I know, I know, I hear you! "I hate paperwork; sitting down and doing all that planning. Plan, plan, plan. Burning the midnight oil. Let me get out of here and sell! I'm a salesperson!"

I know you are. And let's hope a good one. But you have to plan! In the thirty years I've been in selling I have never met a long-term successful salesperson that hasn't *planned it that way!* It's like any business. If you were running a corner store and all you did was open the door in the morning and close it in the evening, you wouldn't have much of a business would you? You have to keep records. Keep a check of the stock. Take a note of what is selling. What's profitable and what isn't. You would have to calculate ways of advertising and methods of marketing to bring people into your store. What about paying the rent and perhaps even wages? Once you start keeping records so that you know what activity achieves results and what is a loss maker, then you can use these records to plan! Plan to do the right things at the right time and in the right quantity. It's no good to saying, "Well here I am with a store full of stock. Here we go!" You'll go broke! Many do!

So planning is the way to steer you in the right direction and allow you the time to do those things that are profitable.

Planning is not a burden, it is a relief from a burden!

The more you plan the easier the job will be because you will start doing those things that make you successful, and only those things.

What a relief it would be to actually know that your activity is going to make you a profit! Not might. *Will!*

That's what planning can do for you. Take the time to sit down and plan you life. You know *you can actually design your life!* Don't just plan your next vacation. Plan your career!

What kind of things should you plan? Anything to do with your business. I've seen people plan to get up an hour earlier than usual in order to study their business and improve themselves, and the difference has been remarkable.

Plan to exercise. Plan to relax, and plan your work.

If you don't know what to plan then start keeping records and find out. You must know what a referred lead is actually worth for instance. If you don't know this basic piece of information then you can't possibly know how many you should be getting can you?

What is a phone call to get an appointment worth? Don't know? You must! What is an appointment worth? These are the building blocks of your business and you have to understand them.

To enable us to fill our 'in tray' correctly we have to know what to put in it and what to leave out. I remember a salesperson that made many morning appointments. He saw more people in the morning than at any other time and yet when we analysed his work we discovered that most of his sales came in the afternoon. In fact it was between the hours of 2 pm and 4 pm that eighty percent of his sales came.

When we pointed out this simple fact and changed his

method of appointing by asking for more appointments in the afternoon, his production almost doubled.

Had he taken the trouble to keep proper records on which to build his plan he would have succeeded far sooner.

Record keeping is therefore essential to the selling process because without it we can't hope to take corrective action when needed, nor will we have the knowledge to streamline our activity in such a way that we only use those activities that are profitable.

Successful people do the things that failures don't like to do and *failures don't like to plan!*

It's as though they are frightened to plan in case they fail!

Record keeping and planning go hand in hand. Sometimes it's difficult for us to know what records to keep because we don't know what will be valuable for us or not. My advice would be to write down most things that you do in your business and link that information to the results you have achieved. By doing this over a reasonable period of time you will begin to see a picture emerging. You will begin to understand what part of your activity pays, how much it pays and when it pays. You will also begin to understand (and this is vital information for salespeople) that *the only thing you get paid for is your* **activity.**

If you doubt me stay inert for a while and see how much money you make. The state of inertia is without doubt the worst place to be. Almost any other state is better than the state of inertia, even the state of panic! At least in panic you are active and what do we get paid for? Our activity! By keeping proper records of our activity and results we begin to understand our business, work more efficiently, which means more profitably.

I sometimes ask a classroom of beginning salespeople to imagine they are sitting at their desk inert. Beside them is a conveyor belt with piles of money on it. The conveyor belt points towards their pocket. As long as they remain still so will the belt. Now they reach out to pick up the phone to make an appointment.

Before their hand even touches the telephone the conveyor belt starts moving, moving slowly and "chink chink" money starts falling into the person's pocket. They pick up the phone and the belt speeds up ever so slightly "chink chink".

They dial the number "chink chink" a little faster. They speak into the phone and make an appointment, or not, and "chink chink" the money falls into their pocket and even if the person says 'no' the money stays there.

Nobody can take it away *because you get paid for your activity.* You have done something towards their business to make a profit and by keeping records you can cost that activity.

Appointing.

One of the most difficult parts of this job of selling (so they say) is making the appointment, to get the prospect to agree to see you. I believe the problem arises because so many of us are frightened of being sold something we don't really need. It's quite normal for people to feel this way and one of the obstacles that we salespeople have to overcome. Sometimes we succeed and at sometimes we don't.

It's the law of averages! What we have to do is try and get the *odds in our favour—the bias our way.*

We have already discussed approachability using the referred lead method. This to a very great extent gives us something of an edge. We now have to couple this with a workable and reliable approach.

When we approach a prospect with the idea of getting an appointment, what is it do you think, you are selling? Would you be trying to sell the product for instance? Many salespeople think so. Would it surprise you to know that the product is the last thing you should be trying to sell when trying to get an appointment.

What we are actually attempting to convince the prospect to do is give us a chunk of his or her time to allow us to meet so that we can show the benefits of our product or service.

You can't sell when the scene is not right. You can't sell 'out of bounds'. Over the years I've seen so many so called salespeople standing in passageways trying to sell. Sitting in bars or restaurants trying to sell. Sitting in crowded offices with no privacy, trying to sell. The fact is, no matter how good you are, it can't be done!

One of the most important lessons a beginning salesperson must learn is to make sure that when they start their sales presentation the conditions are right. Will there be interruptions? Is this the right person? The decision maker? Have you been allocated enough time? Are the physical conditions good enough? Space, desk or table, privacy and so on?

Unless the conditions are right why start selling? You would be wasting your time.

So a part of planning is to think ahead to try to see the possibilities good or bad and try to get the odds in your favour. The *bias* your way!

Plan ahead all the time. So that when the time comes to deliver your presentation you know that everything is going to be okay.

This is not always easy, but a little careful questioning can work wonders. Remember I said salespeople are good 'askers'? This is one time you must ask.

As an example say:

"When could we sit down and spend an hour together with no *interruptions so that I can show you what I have in mind?"*

Sounds like it's important doesn't it? And it is, if your product is as valuable to him as you believe. Don't accept second best as if you were just another salesperson. You are not! You are valuable to your prospect even if at first he or she may not think so. You can't change their mind in five minutes. It takes a full presentation to do that and a full presentation must be done *'in bounds'*, in the right circumstances.

If you fail at this you will fail with the rest of it. Don't be afraid to say,

"We can't talk here John, why don't we make another time so that I can show you exactly what I have in mind. Would your office or mine suit you best?"

By refusing to talk about it now, you have kept the lid on the 'curiosity box' and curiosity can be a powerful motivator. It is responsible for most of the advances that mankind has made. If we weren't curious we would never have progressed!

The curiosity box.

Let's suppose that I were to show you a box. This box is about 30cms sq. and it is gift-wrapped. I say to you,

"In this box is something so valuable, that if you didn't have it you would give all you possessed to get it and it's right here in this box!"

Curious? You bet! I wonder what could be in the box? Now you take the box from me and eagerly tear it open. What is inside? Nothing! Nothing? How can this be? You said it was something valuable, and so it is. There was air in the box and without air we would all die!

What happened to your curiosity level? High for a start? Then dropping low when curiosity is satisfied. Our job as salespeople is to *keep the lid on the curiosity box* as long as we can, because in doing so, we are using one of the most powerful emotions in the book. That is why we must not attempt to sell the product until the conditions are right—until we are 'in bounds'. We can only sell the product or service when we know we have a good chance of doing a full presentation and closing the sale. We can't do *that* in a crowded office, a bar or when the prospect is not the decision maker and above all when we have too little time.

When a prospect asks us to tell him a little about it now, we must be strong and resist all temptation to comply and in so doing we keep the lid firmly on the curiosity box. The box should only be opened when the time is right and even then *it must be opened slowly,* not ripped open but carefully unwrapped, a little bit at a time, until your product or idea is revealed with all it's benefits on view to dazzle our prospect...*That's selling!*

So how do we get somebody interested enough to give us an appointment? Well as we have seen, we have to keep the curiosity level high and at the same time maintaining a low level of information. Keep the facts out of it and the *possibility* of benefits up front.

What do I mean by this? Supposing I said to you,

"I have got an idea for you which knowing you as I do would be of great benefit to you, if used in the right way."

You would say. "What is this idea?"

"Well we don't have time now to discuss it in detail and I don't have the necessary information to hand. What about we make a time tomorrow to look at it?"

You might say, "Just tell me a brief outline of it. Is it to do with my job?"

"Let's wait until tomorrow. Would the morning or afternoon be better for you?"

Are you curious? Of course you are! And the chances are you would grant me an appointment. You might even be anxious to see me!

When we meet it will be my job to open the curiosity box *slowly and interestingly.*

Most approaches to gain an appointment are made on the 'phone. It's quicker and cheaper than calling on a prospect to ask for an appointment. On the 'phone we are just a voice. Now this is good—and bad. It's good because it gives us all an equal opportunity to sound interesting and *people won't be interested unless we are interesting!* On the 'phone there are no distractions, he or she doesn't know what we look like, only what we sound like and with a bit of practice we can sound brilliant!

It's bad because we can't use body language to help us sell, and let's face it he may wish to talk about it now and the circumstances could be right. So we have to weigh up the pros and cons.

I still think that the 'phone is better because you can talk to more people in less time. *Nearly everyone you want to meet is on the end of a 'phone somewhere.* We just have to find out who and where. Then make the call and ask for the appointment.

The telephone approach I am going to give you works! It's been my standard approach for years and I can guarantee that it will work for you if you learn it and use it properly.

We already know that nothing in selling works 100% of the time. What we are trying to do is get the odds in our favour and then do whatever it is enough times, so that those odds will work.

If you took the worst approach you could think of, "You wouldn't want to buy such and such today would you?" and did it enough times, eventually someone will say "yes". But there are better ways! There have to be 'no's' in there somewhere, but lets keep them to a minimum shall we?

Firstly we have to sound interesting without actually telling anything about what we are selling. Remember the curiosity box? Now this may not be entirely possible, depending on what it is you are selling. It may be that you *do* have to tell a little bit about it. But the key word is *little!* If you disclose too much, curiosity will be satisfied and interest will die. If interest dies, the prospect won't want to see you. So you must be strong.

Here then, is an approach that works. If it doesn't quite suit your business, change it around a bit to suit you.

Mr. Brown?

'Yes.'

Mr. John Brown?

'That's right..'

John (or Mr. Brown.) my name is...(your name)...of.... (your company.)

I wonder has Jim Smith mentioned my name to you recently?

'Yes' or 'No'.

*John, I was talking to Jim recently showing him an idea that he found **very interesting and valuable**. During our conversation, I asked him for the names of the most successful people he knows in (your town) and he mentioned your name.*

John, so that we can get together and discuss this idea, are morning or afternoon appointments best for you?

Reply could be, Morning or Afternoon, or he may have a question. 'What's this idea all about?' Here you must keep the lid on the curiosity box. Be very general.

John, this idea is in regard to more efficient operation in your office.

saving tax on your income

increasing profitability in your company

making better use of your leisure hours.

Naturally you must make the phrase suit your business. <u>But as soon as you have said it and without drawing breath say,</u>

Would you be free for a short time tomorrow at 10:00 a.m. or would 2:30 p.m. be better?

He will now give you a time or give you an objection. Objections can only fall into one of a few categories

NOT INTERESTED. *" I can understand you not being interested in an idea that you haven't had a chance to see, but so that you can judge this idea for yourself..."*

Two definite times (see below).

NO MONEY. *"I can understand trying to keep expenses down, and I do think you will find this an interesting and valuable idea."*

Two definite times (see below).

NO TIME. *"I know how busy you are John, that's why I called rather than just call in to see you."*

Two Definite times (see below)

NO NEED. *"I can understand you saying that John, but so that you can judge this idea for yourself..."*

Two Definite times (see below)

Two Definite Times.

"Would you be free for a short time at..................or would..................be better?"

Always, always end with the choice of two times hanging in the air!

It has been my experience that as long as you end your part of the conversation with a choice of two *definite times,* your ratio of calls to appointments will be what it should be.

Don't forget to keep a record of your 'phone activity and your results.

When you talk to somebody on the 'phone, *slow down;* speak at about half your normal speed so that your prospect can catch up with what you are saying. Speak clearly and smile. You can actually hear a smile, *and you must practice!* Make sure that you know your 'phone presentation so well that you don't have to worry about what you are going to say. After a while you will notice that most prospects behave in a similar way and say much the same things. You won't win them all, but by using the right techniques, you will certainly get your share.

What if your prospect is not referred? Does it mean you can't use the telephone? Certainly not! You merely have to alter your opening statement slightly.

"Mr. Brown my name is...............of...............has anybody mentioned my name to you recently?"

"No."

"I've been doing a lot of work with people in your business (or area) lately, showing them an idea that has proved to be very helpful.

John, are morning or afternoon appointments best for you?"

Then carry on in the normal way.

Before you start your telephone session, make sure you have the list of prospects you are going to contact and mark in your diary or planner when you intend to make appointments. It is then a simple matter of going to your diary and asking for a choice of times that suits you. Always give yourself a definite objective regarding how many appointments you want to make and don't stop until you have achieved your goal. If you get it easily and quickly why not carry on and see how many you can get if you *really* try? That's what makes successful sales people.

If on the other hand, if you find that things are not going too well *don't give up!* Persistence makes for success. If you do the things successful people do, guess what you become?

Once you have achieved your target, get out a note pad and write a confirmation note to the appointed prospect and mail it straight away!

Something like,

Dear John,

Thanks for showing interest in my service.

I look forward to meeting you 10:00a.m. Wednesday 3rd

Yours sincerely,

You would be surprised how many times people will thank you for the forethought of confirming the appointment. It serves to make you more of *a real person* in their eyes.

If you are dealing mainly with referred leads, never forget to get back to the nominator of the leads and thank him or her for their help. Even if no business resulted, you should say,

"Thank you John for allowing me to see these people. As it happens I was unable to be of service to them just now, but I'm sure it will lead to other business."

Don't be surprised if he or she offers you some more leads because you are probably the first person who has ever taken the trouble to get back with thanks.

If the calls did result in business, say so. Naturally the details of any business done, should remain confidential, so you could say,

"John, I was able to help Michael and I'm delighted to say he is

now my client. So you have really helped him—and me! Thank you very much. How about lunch on Thursday?"

You never know you could be building a centre of influence! It's all a part of planning. Planning your day. Planning your week. Planning your life!

You are in charge of your own activity and as such are able to control your own success. People don't fail in selling; they just cease doing those things that successful people do!

When I was starting out in selling and—as happens to every salesman sometimes—I fell into a slump, I would say to myself, *what would a successful salesman do?* and before too long I was back on track, because to be successful we must do those things that successful people do.

I believe that some people fail because they would rather not put in, what they perceive to be, an effort. They would rather have the 'easy' life. I feel so sorry for these failures. They haven't realised that, in fact, *it is easier to be successful!*

When one balances the so called 'easy' life—of not working hard, when it's time to work, of not having to plan and keep to a schedule, of not having to take the knock-backs and the disappointments that are an inevitable part of a busy salesperson's life—against the kind of life in which you are busy and productive. Where you have more than enough to pay your bills. Where there is joy in going to work and coming home to a beautiful house in a suburb that you choose, driving a nice car and having great vacations every year, then most of us would see that *to be successful is much easier than failing!*

Successful people are free—poor people are not!

Anyone *can* be successful—not everyone *will*.

Planning is a vital part of your success; it makes the difference between rich and poor.

My advise to anyone who seriously wishes to make a

go of a selling career is to firstly, sit down and write a list of the information you need. Information like, what do I want to earn? Not some dream-like amount, but a real objective. Something you can believe, you can see, you can feel and work towards. Then you must analyse your activity to find out what it is worth.

Make a list. You need to know:—
1. What is a 'phone call worth?
2. What is an appointment worth?
3. What is a presentation worth?
4. What is a referred lead worth?

Make a list, build on that list and only then will you have the database which will tell you what amount of *activity* it is necessary *to achieve your goals*. Then put your head down and enjoy your work in the full knowledge that you will and must be paid for that activity!

The Law of Averages.

We have all heard the expression, 'it's a numbers game', and so it is, but then, so are most endeavours. It really doesn't matter what it is you are trying to achieve, you must have the numbers to back you up. Picasso couldn't have been a famous artist just by painting one work of art, no matter how good it might have been! You have to have the numbers so that any judgement is based on enough statistics. You can't plan an accident prevention program, if all the information you have to base your program on, is one accident. It can't and won't make any sense. In the same way, we as salespeople have to have the requisite number of events on which to base a firm course of action.

Let's look at *closing interviews* as one activity to analyse. A *closing interview* is one in which you have tried to close the sale, in other words the prospect has had an opportunity to buy the product or service. We will assume that over a period of time you have made sixteen *closing interviews* and made four sales.

You further discover that your commission for each sale is $800.

OK so far? Well let's step back a bit and view what we have with a bit of objectivity. Firstly it is **inevitable** that there will be a ratio of no's to yes's. There is no world where you achieve yes's all the time. If there were, *you* wouldn't be required. We would just need a number of order takers, and order takers don't earn vary much money.

So bearing in mind the *inevitability* of the no's amongst the yes's, shouldn't we take *them* into our calculations? It would seem good sense to recognise the no's as being just as important, just as real, and in many ways *just as acceptable* as the yes's!

Surely then, we should be going out looking for no's just as keenly as we look for yes's. Not only that *we should be thankful for them!* In most cases we get more no's than yes's, and if we are going to look upon them as a negative, we will lose heart and become negative towards our job and ourselves. This would be wrong thinking!

No's are to be welcomed!

Why? Because they earn us money! That's why! Let's rearrange our thinking a bit. First of all *the sale is not worth $800.* That was the end result of our *activity* for which we got paid, *not just the yes's!* The *no's* were not worthless; they caused us eventually to get a *yes.*

So we had sixteen *closing interviews* and earned $3200. Doesn't that mean that every *closing interview* was worth $200 *whether the prospect said 'yes' or 'no'?* Of course it does! We should thank those people that say 'no' to us, because they have earned us money. They have earned us money just as surely as the people who said 'yes'.

The trick is in knowing *your own* ratio so that you can plan your activity in such a way that you earn what you want to earn. This applies to all your activity, 'phone calls, referred leads, face-to-face approaches and so on. Then we can really understand planning for what it is, a *road map*, built upon correct information, a map that will lead to our eventual success. After all, isn't that what we all want in life, success?

4.
The Presentation.

Now it's all very well talking about planning, prospecting and appointing, but there comes a time when you have to start *presenting*. That means the time has to come when we have to sit down with the prospect and present our idea, product or service. Do I hear an impatient sigh of relief? After all isn't this what selling is all about?

It sure is! Many salespeople find this the most satisfying and easiest part of the sales process and in many ways it is. Once you know how to present and your product stands up to scrutiny, it certainly can be the most enjoyable part of selling.

The presentation is crucial to your success in selling because it is the presentation that the prospect buys! Some people take issue with this proposition, arguing that if they are selling a tangible product such as a motorcar, then the buyer sees the car, drives the car, likes the car and buys the car. To some extent this is true but only to *some* extent. If the salesperson is not on their wavelength and makes comments that are negative to the sale, then no matter how much the prospect likes the product he or she will, more than likely, turn away.

Many years ago a colleague of mine owned a beautiful pig skin briefcase. It was one of those very professional looking ones that carried papers, zipped up on three edges and was carried under the arm. It was very smart and had that kind of patina that only a quality product achieves with time. I asked my friend where he had purchased it and he told me. I made my way to the store and approached the 'salesman' behind the counter.

On the shelf behind him I saw the exact item.

"I'd like to see that briefcase behind you please." I said. He looked up at the briefcase and then at me, paused and said, "It's very expensive!" "Oh!" I said.

"Have a look at this one." and he showed me another one, a black one, quite unlike the one I wanted. "It's got more pockets, it's made of black leather so it won't mark as easily, and above all it's cheaper!"

I suppose he imagined that this was a good sales-pitch. I stared at him for a long time, and just as he was about to speak again, I said, "No thanks!" turned on my heel, and walked out the store. I never did buy that pigskin brief case. We all need to be sold!

I believe that a salesperson's job is to *find out what the customer wants and sell it to him!* Surely that is our purpose. Not to sell him what *we* want to sell.

Ask questions.

It took me quite a long time, when I came into selling, to learn one of the most important lessons regarding this fascinating craft, and that lesson was to *ask questions.* Remember I said all great salespeople are great askers? And so they are. Every time you are in danger of making a statement, see if you can turn it into a question. Why? So that we get the prospect's brain ticking over. You can rest assured that *it is the prospects brain that does the buying,* and unless it does we won't get very far!

So an important part of the presentation must be devoted to asking questions. To illustrate this point lets compare two methods of trying to sell someone on the idea of saving money in the long term.

"John, if you regularly take a little bit of you money out of what you earn now, and send it on ahead, then you will have money when you retire. You will be able to go where you please, when you please, knowing you will never be a burden to anybody. Of course, if you don't save anything, you will be broke, having to rely on social security to live."

Now all these statements are true and they are all to the point, in fact one could say that they are fairly persuasive. But the problem is, *they are all statements,* and our prospect could easily let these statements go over his head to disappear forever. Communication is a two way street. Not only must we develop an idea, *that idea must be received,* and one of the best ways, if not the only way, is to ask questions! Now lets look at the correct way to get the idea of long-term savings across.

Question:

"John, if you never save any money at all between now and your age of retirement, how much will you have?"

Answer: "Not much."

Question: *"Is that what you want?"*

Answer: "No."

Question: *"Then what do you want John?"*

Answer: "I want some money."

Question: *"How are you going to accumulate it?"*

Answer: "I suppose, by saving it?"

Question: *"John, when do you think is the best time to start?"*

Answer: "Well er...now."

You see the difference? You see how much more powerful asking questions is, when compared to making statements?

Whenever you are in danger of making too many statements in your presentation stop, think and turn them into questions. Every time your prospect answers one of your questions, he is giving a little of himself to you, and each time this happens, you are learning more about the way he or she thinks, and that information will always show you ways to make the sale.

So in designing your presentation make sure you get the prospect to start thinking, to open up and to help you to sell. *Practice turning statements into questions,* they are a lot more interesting. Statements are facts, and facts are a bit like onions, by themselves they don't taste too good. You have to mix them up with other things. Facts have to be mixed with questions.

Most buying decisions are emotional.

The decision is nearly always based on *want* rather than *need.* There are times of course when need *is* the driving force, but in most cases you can bet that your prospect can be motivated by *wants.* They say that logic (facts) can open the mind, but it is *emotion* that will open the chequebook,

The range of human emotion is infinite and powerful. It is emotion that guarantees the continuation of the human race. It is emotion that gives us the world's great works of art and the wonderful inventions that we take for granted every day. Emotions such as love, hate, pride, greed, fear and despair can be broken down into any number of shades, colours and meanings. We, as salespeople need to have a basic understanding of the emotional impulses that drive us.

Let's put this concept of emotional drive to the test and see if it is true.

Peter wants to buy a new car; his old one has just about had it, and so he starts looking around for a new replacement. He decides on certain criteria such as number of doors, size of engine, economy, performance, colour and so on. There are a number of makes and models that suit these criteria are in Peter's price bracket.

Naturally, he visits a number of dealers who all show him the features of their particular vehicle. He tests drives a number of cars to get a feel of what they will do for him and his family. He discovers that these new cars are technically excellent, to such an extent that they are all very much alike. Logically, any one of them will do the job. But something is missing. Just 'doing the job' isn't quite enough for Peter. It doesn't 'hit the spot'. He begins to get a feeling of *unexcitement* (if there is such a word).

One day Peter is talking to an old friend and mentions the fact the he is going to buy a new car. He has looked at all the different models and can't seem to make a decision. Now it just so happens that his friend is something of a car fanatic and suggests to Peter that he abandon the idea of buying a new car. He knows of a car, not new, that would suit him down to the ground. This car is five years old but in 'beautiful condition'. To buy this car *new*, would cost twice the price of any of the new cars Peter is looking at. It is, after all, a 'prestige' vehicle. It has leather upholstery, walnut veneer trim and so on and so on.

Peter takes a drive. He notices that the petrol consumption is a little high and on enquiry finds out that the insurance is more than normal, the tyres are expensive and the engine, if it ever went wrong, would cost a fortune to fix. But Peter is 'sold'. There is something about the way this vehicle drives, something about the way this car handles *and something about the way it makes him feel!*

Peter buys the car.

Is this logical? Is it something his accountant would approve of? No Sir! This is completely and absolutely *emotional!*

Perhaps it was the way that people looked at him as he drove passed. It may have been the way it made him feel, (The quietness, the ride, the smell.) It may have been that although the car was five years old, it had a feeling of 'quality' about it, of permanence.

The new cars lacked what the older car had. They all did the same job in the same way and yet there was an indefinable quality that sold Peter on this other car. Emotional? Of course! When one tries to define it, it slips away. It could be, that Peter enjoyed the sensation of being 'above the crowd'. What ever it was, we will only be able to say it was a decision based on an *emotional stimulus.* Not logic!

It stands to reason therefore that if we are going to design a workable presentation, it must contain emotional stimulus.

A real estate salesman notices, that while he is showing a young couple a house, the wife loves the garden, and in particular a big old tree in the back. The husband, on the other hand is concerned about access to public transport, which isn't very good. Every time the question of public transport comes up, the salesman acknowledges the fact and then talks in glowing terms about the garden, the tree, and how they would enjoy summer evenings in the garden in the shade of the old tree. How the birds would come, attracted by the tree, and how it takes so long to establish a garden of such character. They buy! Not a house, *but a garden!*

We salespeople have to learn to sell the sizzle not the steak. We have to take the facts and turn them into benefits. Now there's a word! Benefit! People don't just buy a product, they buy what they believe it will do for them. It stands to reason therefore, that salespeople need to have the ability to stir the emotions of others, to get inside their heads and make them feel something. Because *emotions have to do with feeling, not thinking.* Emotion is the internal engine that drives us all.

What if you were selling insurance? There is probably no person in that industry that knows as much about the product and how it works, than the actuary. He is the person who designs the product in the first place. He is a mathematician. It is the actuary that calculates all the figures to take into account the needs of the insured as well as the needs of the insurance company, based on all the probabilities. He understands all the premiums, the charges, the limitations and the payouts. He has the mathematical expertise to calculate to the nth degree, future outcomes. He ends up with the 'perfect' product that takes into account life expectancy, as well as the effect certain illnesses have on longevity. To be an actuary takes a long time and involves a lot of study. Most of the actuary's knowledge is based on logic, and rightly so! But the facts alone don't sell policies, and *the actuary is one of the last people you would choose to go out and sell.* The very skills required to calculate the many different parts of a policy are almost diametrically apposed to the same skills required to go out and sell the same policy! The actuary knows more about the policy than anyone and yet if he were to go out and share this vast knowledge with people, he would make no sales.

You see *people are not so much interested in what it is, as to what it will do for them.* What is in it for them? *They are not so much interested in how it works, as how it performs.* They want to know what it will do for them, not how it does it!

The salesperson's job is to paint pictures in the mind of

the prospect that enables the prospect to see and feel what it would be like to use the product, enjoy it, benefit from it and savour the sizzle not the steak.

That doesn't mean that the salesperson doesn't need to have product knowledge, he does! The salesperson must be able to answer each and every question that is asked of him. If he can't, then his credibility will be shot to ribbons! Product knowledge is very important, but in the overall sales presentation, it is not *the* most important thing. It needs to be there but let's not flaunt it. You'll find that if you are too anxious to air your knowledge about the product, the prospect will mentally switch off, particularly if he is not too familiar with the subject.

I recently bought a notebook computer and discovered that because I was asking questions about the product, I was being hammered with facts at such a rate, I was completely unable to understand them. It took me some time to get around the bits, bytes, RAM's and ROM's of most computer salespeople, to find someone who would actually tell me *what it would do for me*. I know this sounds hard to believe, but *not one* salesperson asked me what I wanted a computer for, what I was going to do with it, how often I was going to use it, would anyone else be using it, would it stay in the same place and had I used one before?

Incredible isn't it? You see the answer to these questions tells the salesperson how he can sell me. Once you can find out what a person wants you are well on the way to making a sale. You have to be a great asker! Sound familiar?

Let the prospect participate.

One of the great advantages that salespeople of tangible products have is that many times they can get the prospect involved in a very real way, with the product. The prospect can drive the car or play the organ or listen to the CD. He can try the computer game or swing the golf club or tennis racquet.

The problem is a little more difficult to solve if you are selling an intangible. When I first came into selling I was selling life insurance and I watched as salespeople scribbled numbers on pieces of paper in front of the prospect. Many times it was difficult for the prospect even to *see* the numbers let alone understand the product or what it would do for him. I think it's all to do with two-way communication.

Just because we are giving (or think we are giving) the information to the prospect, the prospect may not be *receiving*, and by writing a lot of figures down in front of the prospect we have no way of knowing if he or she is receiving. I believe the same thing applies today with the small computers that some salespeople use to show facts and figures. There is still no way of knowing if we are getting through, even if the prospect is given a printout.

Many years after coming into the business, I designed a presentation that enabled the prospect to write down his own figures and do his own calculations. He was actually taking part in the presentation. The results of this method were very exciting; the mere act of writing something down guarantees that at least the prospect is getting the message, *your message*. We still use this very simple technique today, and shun 'computer presentations'.

The only way I would ever use a computer to present an idea would be to invite the prospect to punch the buttons and still write down his own results. Information must not only be given, it must be received! By getting the prospect to write his own solution, you are not only helping him to understand, you are also impacting on his memory, so that if he has to take some time to make a decision, and perhaps compare your ideas with those of the opposition, he has a greater chance of remembering yours, because he wrote it down!

I would recommend the many investment advisers out there who are so keen on giving people computer read-outs to try this simple method. The results will be startling.

It is clear, therefore, that a prospect must be given an opportunity to actively take part in the presentation. If your particular product or service doesn't have any figures to write down, you might try some diagrams, which have a multiple choice factor, so that the prospect can point out, or choose, his preferences. Try to find something for the prospect to do, and in that way, you will avoid giving a 'lecture'. If calculations are involved, ask the prospect to punch the calculator buttons and read out the result. The days have long gone when a prospect sits down and receives a 'sales talk' from a 'slick' salesperson. If I had to choose something I have learned over the years that has had more effect on my success than anything else, it would be to let the prospect participate in the sale! It allows you to get your points across in the best possible way.

Listening.

Have you ever been in conversation with somebody and had the feeling they weren't listening? There is nothing more deflating is there? There you are telling this person all about what you consider interesting and wham! Suddenly you realise that he is not there! His mind has gone walkabout. I'll bet you've been guilty of that same crime.

Listening is one of the most important parts of communication. Do I hear some people saying, "But I do listen. I'm a good listener!"

Most of us think we are, and I suppose, in the normal course of events we listen just as well as the next person. (One ear on the conversation and the rest of the brain planning to say something important as soon as we get the chance). We as salespeople can't afford to be 'casual' listeners. We have to be better than that.

To listen *effectively* we have to listen *actively* and let the other person know you are listening. When your prospect is talking, look him right in the eye and follow his words carefully. Watch his body language, note *how* he says things as well as *what* he says. When he has finished talking, make sure he really has finished.

"Is there anything else you would like to say?"

Encourage him to talk and let him know you are a listener! You never know, you could be the first person in a long time that has actually taken the trouble to listen to what he has to say—and want to know more.

Use phrases such as, *"A moment ago you said...Now that was interesting because.."*

He will think, "This person is really taking notice of what I say".

One of the easiest ways to get people to like you is to listen to them and give credit for their ideas and statements. All of us could benefit by checking our listening behaviour. Next time you are in conversation, make a conscious effort to listen more that you talk. Encourage the other person to speak, and when you ask a question, take the trouble to listen carefully to the answer. You never know, you may discover that everything your prospect says is a stepping-stone to another sale! He will, in effect, be telling you how you can sell him!

One of the advantages of having a prepared presentation and learning it very well, is that you have no real need to think about what to say next. You *know* what comes next and this gives you a great opportunity to listen actively to your prospect so that you will be able to 'tune in' to his thought patterns and adjust your presentation to suit. You can't understand another person's motivations unless you understand a person's thinking.

In the relatively short time we have with a prospect, we must find out as much as we can about what 'turns him on'.

Please don't think that I am advocating losing control of the presentation. I'm talking about *controlling* it! Sometimes a prospect gets so enthusiastic about being listened to, he will get right off the track. This is okay to some extent because we want him to feel comfortable, but there must come a time when we have to steer the conversation back to where we want it. How? By asking questions. Questions that will bring him back to the point.

"John, you said that it was important to you to have access to information at all times. I wonder, how wide a spread of information are you including here?"

Notice that this is an open-ended question, by that I mean one that can't be answered by a simple 'yes' or 'no'. The prospect has to think about the answer. Has to do a little mental checking; to marshal his thoughts; to come back to the point of the discussion, and that is what we want him to do. Remember this poem?

I had six honest serving men,
They taught me all I knew,
Their names are what? and why? and when?
and where? and how? and who?

Any question starting with one of these six words cannot be answered 'yes' or 'no'. Try it. Practice asking open ended questions and you will certainly learn a lot more about the person you are talking to—if you listen to the answers.

A few years back we asked a team of sales people to go out into the market place, office buildings, industrial area and so on, not with the idea of selling anything, but just to meet people. The idea was to allow new salespeople to get used to talking to strangers.

They were instructed to introduce themselves using a business card and ask for a few moments of time. The way it went was like this,

"Mr. Jones, I have often been past your business door and promised myself that one day I would find the time to come in and say 'hello', hello! Do you have a few moments now to talk?"

The answer naturally is 'yes' or 'no'. If it was 'yes', then the new salesperson was instructed to find out all he or she could about the prospect by asking questions.

"How long have you been here?"

"How are you finding business at the moment?"

"How did you get started in this line of work?"

"Is this your business or are you managing it?"

This list goes on and on.

Because of this exercise we discovered a very curious thing. Most of these salespeople found that they were spending as much as an hour discussing the other person. Most people's favourite topic is themselves and once they were encouraged to talk about themselves they found it very hard to stop. Our salespeople were probably the first people to come through their door who showed a real interest in them. So many people are so wrapped up in themselves, they have no time to be interested in the other person's point of view.

Another amazing fact occurred from this simple exercise. When we contacted the people who had been gracious enough to allow our new salespeople in to see them, they were more than willing to give us an appointment, with a chance of making a sale.

After this experience we trained our people to ask for an appointment at the end of their conversation and it worked. Peoples' favourite topic is themselves. Make no mistake about it!

Knowing now what we do about what motivates people, it is time we discussed the structure of the presentation. All sales presentations follow the same basic configuration no matter what the product or service, and if you are going to design a sales presentation (and I hope you do) then it is just as well that you understand what is involved.

Now before we start on this, I don't want you to run away with the idea that everything is set in concrete. It isn't! A sales presentation is essentially a conversation. An exchange between two or more people that is designed to impart information, enthuse, encourage, solve problems, disturb, close, as well as maintain a positive forward motion at all times. To do all of this properly it is not possible to ad-lib our way to a successful conclusion. There has to be some structure. So lets put down a workable framework to build on.

1. Keeping 'in-bounds'.

One of the most common faults of new salespeople is that they are so keen to make the sale, they will start their presentation at any given opportunity. NO, NO, NO! You must never begin your presentation until you are sure the conditions are right.

a)   Will we have enough time?
b)   Will we have any interruptions?
c)   Will we be private?
d)   Will the physical conditions be right?
e)   Will all the decision makers be there?

First of all you must have sufficient time to make your presentation, answer all the questions, handle any objections and complete the paperwork. What appears on the surface to be a twenty minute sales talk could, in reality, take up to one and half hours. Make sure you are going to have enough time. How do you find out? Ask!

"John, this will take about an hour to run through; will that be okay?"

Interruptions of any kind can kill a sale. Try as far as you are able to cut them out. Ask your prospect to ask his secretary to put any incoming calls on hold. Alternatively pick a venue where interruptions will be unlikely. I've made many sales in my own office—where I'm in control. Privacy is important to your presentation. You don't want other people listening in to you. They are not involved and yet they can make comments detrimental to the sale.

By 'physical conditions' I mean, is there somewhere to sit? Can you spread your papers out so that your prospect has every chance of understanding your message? Can he sit with you and partake in the conversation?

Decision makers are the ones who are competent to make the buying decision. Not everyone will buy something without talking it over with someone else first, and rightly so. Therefore you must ensure that you have everyone who will be involved at the presentation.

When I was selling life insurance, I would talk to the husband during business hours, only to discover that there was no way he was going to make a decision until he had discussed it with his wife, and no matter how good I was, I couldn't break that nexus! So I would say,

"John, where do you live?" (he would tell me) *"I am coming out your way on Monday and also Thursday. Will you be home either of these two evenings?"*

(he would tell me which evening)

"I can't promise anything, but if I get time, I'll call in and we will have a round table discussion and make decisions then."

Now when I went to his home I would do a second full blown presentation for his wife's benefit. Try it. It works!

2. Fact-find

We must have some method of getting the facts that we need to base our discussion on. Sometimes much of this step is done before meeting the prospect for the first time. Sometimes it is during the first time. Sometimes it is during the first five minutes of the presentation and sometimes the fact-find takes place in sections through the presentation. You must decide which is best for your particular business.

For example, it may be that you deal in heavy engineering equipment used in a paper rolling mill. You decided that you want to try and get your product and service into a particular factory.

You would naturally be able to glean most of the information you require before meeting the decision maker.

What are they using now? How long have they had it? What condition is it in? Are there many break downs? What plans have they for the future etc., etc...Much of this information is available through sources other than the main man.

On the other hand, you may be selling investment products to individuals and in this case the source of the information you require must come directly from the prospect himself, at the start of your presentation. You should sit down and design for yourself a fact-sheet that will help you get the details.

Most salespeople need to fact-find even if it is just to ask, *"How can I help you?"* You can't assume anything about the prospect. You must get the facts.

3. Discover the problem

We as salespeople are problem solvers. If there are no problems to solve then we won't make many sales. So once we have the facts we should be in a position to discover and define the problem. It may be that the machinery in the mill is very old and is constantly breaking down causing enormous costs in production.

It may be that an individual has left it rather late to start accumulating funds for retirement and to save enough now is going to cause hardship.

It may be that someone has been looking for a particular item in the stores and has been unable to find it.

Rest assured however, that if there is no problem then there will be no sale.

4. Define the problem.

Most people know they have a problem, and even if they don't, it doesn't mean it isn't there. Our job, after discovering the problem, is to define it. We must, to the best of our ability, put the problem squarely on the table as they say. Expose the problem in such a way that the prospect cannot miss seeing it and cannot help but acknowledge the existence of it. He or she must be able to see the breadth and depth of it and understand it for what it is.

Remember that when we were defining a prospect, one of the qualities was *need?* Well he that has no problem—has no need. But wait, let's not give up so easily, he may still have a *want.* A problem may be subjective; by that I mean, that although we may not think he or she has a problem, *they may think they have!*

Some years ago I was trying to sell a man some life insurance. He had a wife and two children, a mortgage and education expenses looming. Try as I might, I could find no problem. He had everything covered. I was preparing to leave and congratulating him on his foresight, when *he* said, "What about my wife? I want to insure her." No problem? My fault had been in the fact-find which is designed to unearth the problem. *He* knew the problem was there. *I didn't.*

5. Disturb

This is perhaps the most skilful part of the presentation. Unless the prospect is emotionally disturbed about the problem then its no sale.

How do we stir the emotions?

In this regard, a picture is worth a thousand words and in the absence of pictures we have to learn to *'draw'* word pictures. Now some people are better at this than others, but we can all be good! It takes practice. What is a word picture, anyway?

It is when you develop the ability to put the prospect into a situation. He can actually see what is happening, feel the effect and realise, by experiencing the reality of the situation, that unless he takes action (that is the action you want him to take) he will find himself experiencing what you are describing. Don't forget we are talking about disturbing the prospect about his problem. We haven't created the problem, it was there before we walked in. All we have done is define it and disturb the prospect about it.

The important point about this section of the sales process is that if the prospect is not sufficiently worried about his or her problem, then he or she is unlikely to take action to solve it, and solve it they must if we are to make the sale.

The word pictures in this section are not designed to enthuse, (That comes later) they are designed to cause concern. Let me reiterate, we have not caused the problem, only the concern *about* the problem. We have painted the problem so vividly that the prospect cannot deny it exists and if it were possible he would like to solve this problem.

In fact we will ask the question,

"John, if I could show you a way to solve this problem at little immediate cost, would you go ahead?"

It's what we call a trial close and trial closes are sprinkled through any presentation so that we are able to take the prospect's temperature and see how 'hot' he is. Notice that this trial close, like all of them, is a question.

"Would you agree?"
"Isn't that so?"
"Would you say that price is reasonable?"
"I suppose, like most people you are interested in the education of your children?"

and so on. I'm sure you get the picture. Our aim is to get the prospect agreeing with us.

6. Solve the problem.

Now we have disturbed our prospect to the point of wanting to solve the problem surely all we have to do is provide a solution and the sale is made, right? Wrong! Sure, we must provide the solution, but it has to be done in such a way, that *he* perceives the action he has to take to solve it being better for him than putting up with the problem. Many problems can be solved, but if the solution is more onerous than the problem itself, then we might be better off leaving things as they are.

The prospect always has the choice, solve it or not. It is our job as salespeople to make our offering (the solution) more attractive than the problem. The mere fact that he has put up with the way things are until now, could suggest that he is content to keep the status-quo. But you can bet your life that if you have truly disturbed him and enthused him about the solution, you will have a sale!

If your product is designed to solve the prospect's problem, then you can rest assured he is better off with your solution.

It is your *solution* that he eventually buys. But unless the previous steps have been carried out correctly, he may agree that the solution is certainly a good one, but he is not buying. The reason is that he either does no see the problem clearly or is not sufficiently disturbed by it.

You can see, that so far in the presentation we have used logic in defining the problem so that he will open his mind, emotion in disturbing him about the problem, and emotion again in enthusing him about the solution.

7. *Closing*

Closing is the art of getting the prospect to take action—to buy!

I am constantly surprised at how many salespeople take a prospect right up to the line, get him to agree on a solution, even get agreement that he can *afford* the solution, *and then don't try to close.* Nobody can stop you trying! They don't have to buy, but they can't prevent you from trying to close.

I wonder how many sales are missed because we have either assumed we are talking to a non buyer, or we just haven't *summoned up enough courage* to attempt a close.

Many years ago I was privileged to hear a talk given by a man called Carl Bach. Carl had been a salesman for New York Life between the two world wars. He was a Lithuanian Jew and had a thick accent, a bit of New York, a bit of Lithuanian mixed with his own Jewish manner of speech. Carl was about 5ft tall and wasn't much to look at. You would pass him in the street and not know he was anybody special.

Carl wrote life insurance in the tenements of New York, amongst the Irish, Polish, English, German, Russian and other immigrants who had come to America from depressed lands to make their way in the New World! This was a tough territory, these people had little money and Carl sold them the smallest possible policies. You weren't allowed to sell anything smaller! He must have sold a lot of them because incredibility Carl earned $1 million a year!

Yes, this little man with the guttural accent and the lousy territory with the poverty stricken cliental, sold enough business to earn himself a million dollars in one year! This was a salesman! This was a man you had to listen to. He spoke from a position of authority!

I'll never forget the talk that he gave—it was riveting! He must have been over seventy when I heard him, but you could still catch a glimpse of the energy, the enthusiasm and the belief that I am sure impressed his clients and made him the success that he was.

As Carl spoke I began to get a feeling of what it was like to make it on your own, to put up with the hard knocks and come out on top, to start in a strange country and win.

Carl said many things during his talk with us that day, but one statement stood out and has stayed with me ever since. In his strong New York, European voice Carl said,

"Ninety percent of the people you talk to, want to buy what you have to offer!"

I sat there amazed. How could this be? Ninety percent?

My closing rate wasn't nine out of ten and I considered myself to be a pretty good salesman and that means a good closer! So how could I have been so blind to miss so many sales? How could I have got so close to a sale and not felt it? No! It couldn't be right. Not ninety percent! But, you know, over the years, I have thought about Carl Bach and his ninety percent and I have come to the conclusion that *it could be even higher!* We shall be discussing closing a little later when I'm sure Carl Bach will be mentioned again.

7. Getting Referred Leads

Once you have closed the sale, it is just not good enough to leave it there. Whether you have gained a new client or not, you have just lost a prospect! That's right, every time you complete a sales presentation your prospect list is shorter by one and the easiest way to replace that prospect is to ask for referred leads. Make sure you always ask. No one can stop you asking and all good salespeople are great askers.

Build your referred lead presentation into your sales

presentation. Make it an integral part of it and you will succeed in keeping your prospect file full.

The basic structure of all sales presentations therefore is as follows.

1. **In bounds.** You can't sell out of bounds.
2. **Fact-find.** Get all the relevant facts.
3. **Discover the problem.** Nearly everyone has a problem.
4. **Define the problem.** Getting them to understand it.
5. **Disturb.** Making sure they are concerned.
6. **Solve.** Showing them a solution.
7. **Close.** Taking action.
8. **Referred Leads.** Replacing the client with some new prospects.

In most industries, once you have gained a client, after sales service becomes important. Servicing your cliental is building a business, so make sure you have a servicing system built into your work habits. Plan it, write it down and follow through.

5.
Closing the sale.

It is in this area that we can separate the professional from the amateur, the success from the also ran, the rich from the poor and the outstanding from the mediocre. Closing is what selling is all about. It is the essential ingredient that makes us salespeople. Unless we close, or attempt to close, then we are nothing more than educators.

Now don't get me wrong there is nothing wrong with a good education, but by itself it doesn't do very much. It is of value only when its put into practice. A sales presentation is put 'into practice' when a close takes place. Don't go around the world showing everyone how much you know, it won't put dollars in your pocket.

Educating is part of the process, so is enthusing and asking questions and handling objections, they are all part of the process. None of it means anything until a sale is made or we receive a definite refusal to buy.

I like to put it this way,

My reason for being in this sales interview is to fill in the order form. That's right, unless I make an attempt to complete the order form, then nothing of any great importance has taken place. A lot of talk—no sale!

When my eldest daughter Lynn was 3 years old and her sister Marina was just a baby, I decided to buy a well known brand of encyclopaedia, so I filled in a coupon and sent it off.

About two weeks later there was a knock on our front door and there stood a young man with a case in each hand. "Mr. Mansfield?" "Yes." and he introduced himself. I took him into our sitting room and sat him down. He then proceeded to show my wife Elaine and I all the marvellous things about his product.

He had beautiful brochures in full colour, he had a sample of one of the volumes. You could smell the leather, touch the fine paper and see the quality of the print. He told us all about The Book of the Year that updated everything. There were other publications one could purchase, specialising in various branches of science. You could even buy a bookcase to suit the books. What a product! I was sold—or was I?

I remember all the good things about this product but I also remember this young man packing everything away, saying goodbye and walking out the door. What had gone wrong? Why hadn't he closed the sale? I remember asking a few questions. I remember even throwing in a couple of objections. But what I don't remember was saying I didn't want to buy. Strange thing that, he must have assumed it! He must have got some message from me that I did not want his books. So he deprived me of something I wanted!

Echoes of Carl Bach? Ninety percent want to buy? I'll say! My kids were going to have access to all this information as they grew up. Now they weren't! *He walked out with my encyclopaedia!*

Twenty-five years go by. The children grow up and have children of their own. They managed to go through school without the encyclopaedia. Which I suppose says something for *them*. One day I was walking through our local market when what should I see but an encyclopaedia stand. "Fill in your name and address and win a trip to Fiji." Ah ha! I thought.

Here's my chance. I grabbed a card and after filling in the details, dropped it in the slot.

Sure enough, two weeks later there was a knock on our front door and there stood another young man and although it was twenty five years later, he looked like a twin of the first, two bags and all. "Come in!" I said and showed him into our living room.

He sat and proceeded to open his brief cases to show me all the good things about his product.

"You don't need to do all that," I said, "just tell me how much it is."

"Oh no, Mr. Mansfield." he said (You see that is a 'no-no', you must go through the presentation to enthuse the prospect before discussing price.)

"Just let me run through some of the features of this encyclopaedia."

"No thanks, just tell me how much it is." Well he gave in and told me the price.

"Sign me up!" I said.

He must have nearly fallen off his chair. This was the easiest sale he had ever made! He duly signed me up and I gave him the cheque. Two weeks later some boxes arrived and I unpacked my beautiful encyclopaedia. It's great! I use it a lot and enjoy it. I have bought the Year Books each year and find great enjoyment in ownership.

The reason I have told you this story is to point out that *if* that first young man had said something like.

"Rick, there are two ways of doing this, you can pay for the books all at once, up front, which amounts to $................ or you can take advantage of our 12 month interest free budget terms. *Which would you prefer?*" (minor decision) I would probably have said that the 12 months interest free budget terms would suit me best, and if he had then said.

"Fine, Rick what is your full name?" and started filling in the order form, *I would have owned those books over twenty five years ago!*

He deprived me of something I wanted. I was ready to buy but he never took the trouble to close. What a tragedy! All that work and talk for nothing! All that time wasted. I hope *we* never make the same mistake.

Ninety percent of the people you talk to *want* to buy what you have to offer!! If you don't believe that then you have no business in selling. We should explore this ninety percent argument a little further to see exactly what it was that Carl Bach meant.

What did he mean when he said "people you talk to"? Surely not people you talk to casually? People you meet in social situations? People you deal with in business? No. I think he meant those people you talk to about *your* business. Not just your business *in general,* but your business *in particular.* This means, I'm sure, *people who take a full presentation* and get to see and hear the major points about your product.

I think you can safely say that "people you talk to" *means people you try to sell.*

Let's take a scale ranging from zero percent to one hundred percent and place upon that scale, a prospect. We'll assume this prospect is a qualified referred lead, so you have already achieved that all important *approachability.* Because of this, he is up the scale a bit, right from the start. How far would he be ten, fifteen, twenty percent? I would say twenty percent. That means he is already twenty percent of the way there.

You now ring him for an appointment. You use your normal, excellent telephone approach *and you get the appointment!*

Has he gone up the scale a bit? Yes he has. Where does it take him? Thirty percent? Forty? Fifty? I would say forty percent!

Only Sixty percent to go! You go to the appointment and he is there, on time, no excuses about having to go out, no being away due to illness (it happens). He is there to greet you. Up the scale a bit? Yes I think so. To where? Seventy five percent? That sounds OK.

He now takes a full presentation. No interruptions, a few questions, a couple of objections (which you handle) and a number of agreements along the way.

Where is he now? *He has to be up to ninety percent doesn't he?* Either that or he is not a buyer at all (and you should have realised this long before). This means that before you even go into the closing phase of the sales presentation, he or she has a ninety percent chance of *wanting* to buy.

But is he going to say so? No! *You must close!* You dare not assume anything, you must take charge and move into the closing phase of the sale.

What does this mean, I hear you say? How do we do that?

I believe that there is a definite sequence to closing the sale that must be followed if we are going to succeed. Everything is a process. To start the sequence there has to be a closing question and most closing questions ask for an opinion from the prospect.

"Can you think of a better way of saving money?"
"Would this idea help you achieve efficiency in the office?"
"Do you think, that by implementing this training program, you would achieve greater productivity from your staff?"

OK fairly simple so far, and selling *is* simple if we stick to the basics!

Now let's assume that we get a favourable response to our closing question—*an agreement.*

Once we have got this agreement we need a little 'hook' to hang the close on and in this case there is no better 'hook' than a *minor decision.* Remember the encyclopaedia?

"Now Rick, there are two ways of doing this. You can meet the cost up front, which amounts to $....... or you could take advantage of our twelve month interest free budget terms. Which would you prefer?"

A minor decision—easy to make!

By the way, never ask difficult questions of your prospect.

If he can't answer them you will embarrass him. Embarrassed people get angry and angry people don't buy. So keep it simple.

If we get a favourable response to the minor decision we are going to *assume the major decision is carried.* The major decision is, 'yes! I want it!'

Never ask a prospect whether he is going to buy! It is the worst closing phrase in the book.

"Shall we go ahead then?"

NO, NO, NO! NEVER, NEVER, NEVER! Why? Because it is too big a decision. Most prospects will not make that decision and yet most prospects *want to* buy. I know it's strange but it's true.

"Shall we go ahead then John?"

"Well, I'll tell you Rick, I'd better think it over. Give me a few days and I'll get back to you."

I can hear it now, *you have lead with your chin* and you have caught it squarely and deserved it! Make the decision a minor one and all will be well.

As soon as he gives you a favourable response to the minor decision, *you are going to assume the sale.* You are going to behave in the same way as if he had said, "Sign me up!" That's right, he has just said, "I want it, sign me up!" What are you going to do now? Okay, I hear you, I hear you. "I'd sign him up!" Of course you would. But there is an art to that too.

We must be in control of the presentation at all times. At the end of the sale it is normal for a form of some kind to be completed giving details of the product, name of the product, price and so on.

In many cases the prospect has to sign this form for the sale or contract to be completed or agreed to. Always have this form out on the table where the prospect can see it, pick it up, examine it, read it if he wants to. We must, at all costs, avoid pulling out the order or application form like a hidden gun at the end of the sale and frightening the life out of the prospect. Let him get used to seeing it!

At this point in the sales process we must be sure that this form is in front of us, because for the prospect to own the product or service, this form has to be completed. That is *your* job!

We now have the form in front of us, our pen unsheathed, ready for action, and we ask, *"John, what is your full name?"* and we start the physical act of writing the answer to this question, *before he or she has a chance to answer it!* It is called momentum! Of all the important lessons I have ever learned in selling, this is way up there at the top! *Start writing before the prospect has a chance to answer!* You are already writing 'John' as you ask. Now funny things happen in the human brain. You ask the question and proceed to write the answer and their automatic reaction is to help you to complete the answer.

We know of course that nothing works a hundred percent of the time in selling. We are dealing with people, but this *will* work most of the time.

After getting the agreement to our 'minor question' we cannot afford to stop. We have to press on by starting to fill in the order form. Any stopping that is to be done must come from the prospect.

We as salespeople have already made the assumption that he or she wants to buy. If you are going to be successful in selling you must follow this procedure, you don't have any choice, it's compulsory!

Put it this way, if the prospect doesn't stop you, guess what has happened? That's right you have made another sale!

Whilst you are writing on the order form you are naturally going to lose eye contact aren't you? Here I want to make another important point. Very important.

I am not going to look at the prospect again until the form is completed. I have lost eye contact and I'm keeping it that way.

All through the presentation we have been eyeball to eyeball. He has been looking at me. Judging me. 'Can I trust this person? Is he sincere? Is he telling the truth? Can I rely on what he says? Do I like him? Do I want to do business with this person?' I, on the other hand have been watching him very carefully for all kinds of signs, including buying signals. 'Is this person showing interest? Am I holding his attention?' and much more.

Now I'm going to lose eye contact. Why? Well for one thing you can't look at someone and write at the same time, but even when I'm not writing I am going to maintain loss of eye contact. The reason is of course, that it is more difficult for the prospect to say 'no' and to prevent me from filling in the form, if I am not looking him in the eye. He has to almost reach out and grab my arm to stop me. It is much easier for him to answer the question and in most cases, that is exactly what he does.

So you continue to complete the form until you get to the part where the prospect must sign—moment of truth? You bet! Always carry two pens! You don't want to lose control of your pen and he may not have one handy so give him a pen to sign with and don't give him a chewed up old ballpoint!

This word 'sign' can be a problem. The word itself can conjure up some negative thoughts. We have all been told 'never sign anything' at least until you have spoken to your accountant, lawyer, parents or teachers. I am sure we have all heard the horror stories.

'You didn't sign this did you?'

'Yes, why?'

'You really signed it, I can't believe it!'

'Why, what's wrong?'

'Well, you are now guarantor for this money, you could be liable!'

'What, I didn't mean to do that!'

'But you have *signed it!*'

I think we could all recall situations like this, if not regarding ourselves, then regarding other people. So it might be a good idea to avoid the word *'sign'* all together.

After marking where he or she is to sign, I use the term *"Okay this for me, here and here,"* and pass them the pen, (still no eye contact).

Now, when you have had a good meal in a restaurant, you make a sign to the waiter indicating that you wish to pay the bill, he brings it to you, you check carefully and usually, put down a credit card. The waiter takes it away and returns with the credit slip that you have to sign. He then leaves you to it. He doesn't stand over you, waiting for you to sign—not if he is a professional. No he goes away and leaves you alone.

You may want to check the amount again or leave a big tip or leave a small tip or as someone said to me once, you may just want to leave! But seriously, in all cases he will leave you alone to sign. Nobody likes to be watched, pressured or 'hung over' when they are signing something, do they?

So leave him alone. Look for something in your brief case, talk to someone else, write down some figures, what ever you do leave him alone. He may want to read all the fine print. He may want to check what you have written. He may be trying to finally decide if this is the right thing for him to be doing. We will never know what goes through a prospects mind at a time like this and it's not important. What *is* important is that we must not interrupt his thought processes, what ever they are.

If all has gone well he will sign! Make no mistake this is the moment of truth for your prospect-now-client. He has bought your presentation.

Most sales are not made until the money is paid, so we need to get the money. Still without regaining eye contact, ask for the money. If you can offer a choice so much the better.

"Now, John I will need $........will that be cash or cheque?"

Let him answer and start making out the receipt *before you get the money!* Same psychology as before, funny things happen in the human brain, he sees a receipt being made out, his natural impulse is to give you the money to cover it.

Sale made! You live to fight another day! You are a salesperson! Has the interview finished? I hope not. What about referred leads? The raw material of your business. You must replace this new client with some prospects.

In a previous chapter we discussed *how* to ask for referred leads now lets have a look at *when*. What I don't like is this idea that as soon as you make the sale you rush in and ask for referred leads. It's all too rushed, too hurried. I think it is much better to allow a pause to take place between the sale and the referred lead presentation.

There are a number of ways you can achieve this. If the type of selling that you are doing is of a one on one, personal type of selling, you may have been asked if you would like a cup of coffee or tea when you arrived. The thing to do is politely refuse and suggest they leave it until the end of the discussion. It is difficult talking business and drinking coffee at the same time anyway.

Now is the time to suggest a coffee or tea. Even if you weren't offered one at the outset, there is no harm in suggesting it. People love to do things for you. It makes them feel good. "You know John, a coffee would go down well right now. Is that possible?" Most people will leap to their feet to oblige. The idea in using this technique, is that I am trying to break the nexus between being a salesman and a person. I want to become more of a person because I am leading up to asking for referred leads and where, perhaps, some people won't give leads to salespeople, they may oblige *a person*.

During this time I will put him in the picture of what to expect from now on, and if my business is a service business, I will explain when he will see me again and why and how he can contact me should he require any assistance. I try to make a big feature out of my after sales service. In doing this I hope he will be thinking, *"I'm glad I am dealing with Rick Mansfield, he seems to be the kind of person who cares about my problems".*

Don't take too long over this procedure, long enough to make an impact, and when you feel the time is right, look him right in the eye and say,

"John, as you know my business is meeting people and showing them this idea, and I can only do that with your help. You'll help me, will you?"

Then follow the referred lead technique you have already read about. Do it with a will and do it with self expectancy!

Objections.

I hear some people saying, *"All this closing technique is fine, but what happens if the prospect objects?"* Well they do say that the sale begins when the prospect says 'no', and so it does! But don't panic, all is not lost, providing you know what to do! When in doubt, remember Carl Bach. *"Ninety percent of people you talk to want to buy!"* How true. Particularly if you have taken them this far, so have faith. Suppose he stops you right at the closing question?

"In your opinion, John, would this idea help you to achieve more efficiency in your office?"

Answer: "Well it might or it might not, I'll have to think about it and work out in my own mind which way to go".

Wow! Sounds impressive! Sounds business like! Is it? No way! Guess what he is *not* going to do. *He is not going to think about it.* As soon as you walk out that door, bingo, he'll forget you! You see, we know that most of these logical sounding 'objections' are invalid.

So invalid in fact, that if you spend time trying to 'answer' this objection specifically, you run the great risk of talking about something that deep down he knows he is not interested in. *He is not interested in thinking about it.* So why talk about? Let it float away into the 'ether' and talk about the real issue.

What has he really said to you? "I want to think about it?" Not true!

This is what he has said to you and I have proven this over and over again. He said

"Rick, you haven't convinced me yet, keep going and you might convince me. I hope you do because I want it!"

So far the sake of the argument let's assume he *did* say that to you. What would you do?

You would try and convince him wouldn't you? What does he buy? *Your presentation!* So how about we lean on that. How about we take our presentation, and remembering those points in it that caused interest in your prospect, (and if you were watching you would know what they were) we offer to *recap* the presentation..

Recapping answers all objections!

"John, I can understand you feeling that way, many of my clients have said the same thing. (So you are not fighting, you are agreeing) *John, I wonder would you mind* (so you are asking his permission) *if we just quickly recap what we have discussed. Would that be okay?"* Now, depending on the way he answers you will know if he is in the ninety percent that want or the ten percent that don't want. If he answers in a very bored, off hand manner "Alright if you must (yawn)", you are a million miles away from this person, and this sale.

If on the other hand he shows eagerness, "Oh would you mind?" Then you are in with a great chance. So now all you have to do is cover the major points of your presentation as only you can, getting strong agreements along the way, always looking for a chance to say, *"what is your full name…."* with pen poised, ready for action. Don't hesitate, don't be timid, don't be humble. Just do it! It's what we professionals do all the time. It works!

A word of warning. Before you rush into this method of handling objections, you must learn to *relax.* There is nothing worse than a head to head battle with a prospect. No one wins, especially you! So as soon as an objection appears on the horizon, consciously relax. Drop the pen, (you can always pick it up when needed) he sees it as some kind of threat. You are about to do nasty things with it. Like filling out the form. So drop it. Sit back, relax, take a breath, take your time, slow down. Now watch what *he* does. *The same thing!* Yes, he will relax along with you and this makes selling so much easier and more pleasant. No fights. No arguments. Just a friendly helpful discussion. A discussion that leads to a sale. A sale that gives a win-win situation. He has acquired something he wants, and so have you.

Congratulations! Great sale!

6.
Attitude.

The worst bankrupt in the world is the person who has lost his enthusiasm".

There is an expression going around these days referring to 'attitude'. Like 'he's got an attitude', meaning unpleasant or aggressive. But the attitude we are discussing here is more than this. It can be good, bad, indifferent, superior, thoughtful, peaceful, ineffective, positive, negative, creative and everything in between.

Does attitude play much part in our lives? Is it important or not? Where do we get it from? Can it be altered or improved, or are we stuck with it? We have all heard the expression, 'whether you think you can, or you think you can't, you'll be right!' This has something to do with attitude. If we took two sportsmen who were going to compete against each other and one said 'I will win this', and the other said 'I haven't got a chance!' which one would you back? Obvious right?

Attitude is a reflection of the way we think and the way we think is the result of many many factors. Some going right back to our early childhood.

Suppose you were brought up in a very religious family. I bet your attitude to religion would be very strong, whether for or against. Similarly, if you were brought up by free thinking parents, guess what your attitudes to life would be today?

Pretty free? Ever wondered why some people are successful and some fail? I wonder if it has anything to do with attitude? Even more important, I wonder if we could change our life simply by changing our attitude? Wouldn't that be a revolutionary concept—or would it?

They do say that if all the wealth in the world was taken away from the rich people and given to everybody in equal proportions, it wouldn't be too long before it would be back in the same pockets! This will never be proven, but it makes you think?

I wonder if it is the attitude of the people that win 'their' money back that makes the difference. There we were, all equal in wealth and yet those that had been wealthy regain their wealth.

Attitude is something to do with self-image and it is this idea of self-image that holds the key to our behaviour and our actions.

What is your self-image?

How do you view yourself?

Do you see yourself as strong, focussed, goal oriented, energetic and confident? Or perhaps you see yourself as weak, too flexible, letting things happen, lazy and hesitant! If there were two such people, side by side, having equal opportunity, who do you think would win?

Now there is a word, *opportunity!* I don't know whether you can measure opportunity or not. Whether in the scale of things parcelled out to people, opportunity is amongst them. But I do know one thing. *You have to be able to recognise it when you see it!* It's tragic to think about all the missed opportunities that we have had in life. All the times that we could have and didn't. What if we had? Do you know that even if it didn't work out for you, *you would not have been any worse off!* It is all a question of attitude.

Many people ask me what things were like in the selling industry when I came into it over thirty years ago. It's a good question and I try to answer it as best I can. I think about the frustrations, the disappointments, the successes and the highlights. Then I look at new salespeople today and listen to what they tell me, and do you know? I realise that nothing has changed!

Prospects are saying the *same things* that they were then. 'I want to think about it' and 'we never make a decision straight away' and 'I have to talk to my accountant' and 'I want to check the market'. Some of these people weren't even born when I came into selling. *Where do they learn the script?*

It is obvious that nothing has changed. For the last million and more years the sun has come up in the morning and creates daylight and goes down in the evening and it gets dark. It gets hot in the summer and cold in the winter. Nothing has changed. If someone wakes up in the morning, sees daylight and cries out in surprise, *it just means he hasn't been around too long!* It does that every day! And do you know that there is going to be very little change to this order of things in the years to come. You couldn't put the odds on paper to bet for change.

So if it is true, that things will remain much the same physically, industrially and economically, what is going to change? For things to *improve* for you, things must *change* for you? Well, let me tell you what I consider to be a *major truth.* **For things to change for you—you have to change!** You have to get change under your skin. How?

The one thing that you *can* control. The one thing that you *can* change is *your attitude!* If you will change your attitude, *you* will change. It's the only way! It is your attitude that effects your behaviour so that you can work better and more efficiently in an *unchanging environment,* seizing opportunities as they arise. You can do it! It is up to you whether you *will,* but you *can!*

Have you got the will?

Some people might say, "It's alright for you. You've made it. But it's different for me. I didn't get a decent education. I didn't have the kind of parents that encouraged me. I didn't ever have enough money to start something. What hope have I got?" To these people I say "You have got no hope!" If you think your beaten, you are. It's all in the way you think!

I don't pretend to be any kind of psychologist, but I do know some fundamental truths about how we think and behave. After all I'm a salesman.

We all know that we have a conscious and a sub-conscious mind, and it is the sub-conscious that remains a mystery. There are funny things going on in there. Things we don't understand. Strange, dark things. The problem is that it is the subconscious that controls many of our actions. Most of us are carrying around a negative thought or two that may be inhibiting our progress without us even knowing about it.

I believe that we don't necessarily need to know the details of our negativity to have the power to turn it around to positive. It is within our own capacity to use our brainpower to change the way we think.

When I was growing up right up until early adulthood, I had a very bad stutter. It was so bad that my mother would have to give me a written list of items to give the shopkeeper because I found it so difficult to speak and ask for things. School was difficult too, because of the eagerness of teachers to get pupils to read out loud.

I can still feel the bottomless terror I felt then, as it came closer and closer to my turn to read out loud, knowing full well that I was, inevitably, going to make a fool of myself. Yet here I am today selling for a living, training salespeople, managing others and speaking in public. How come? What happened? What made the difference? The difference came fairly early in my life. Having been born in Britain I was required to attend National Service. All young men who had attained the age of eighteen were required to complete two years military service. I elected to go into the air force. My father had been in the Royal Flying Corps in the first world war and my older brother John, was already a fighter pilot. So I thought I would follow the family tradition. Needless to say this was prevented due to my stutter. You can't communicate in a fast moving jet with a stutter, by the time you were able to say anything you would probably have been shot down!

I asked the air force if they would send me for therapy and if I was able to overcome my handicap, could I reapply? They agreed.

It was during these therapy sessions that I began to understand how one could control the mind by getting into the subconscious. Using relaxation to change the way you think.

One of the first things my therapist taught me was to *relax!* Doesn't sound too world shaking does it? Relaxing? What can *that* do for anybody? Surely we all relax, that's no big deal! No, by itself it isn't, after all we all relax when we sleep don't we? And when we sleep we dream. What are dreams but the workings of our subconscious coming to the surface? The problem is, that when we are asleep we don't really have any control over our mind. But what if we could relax and still retain a measure of control over our thought processes? Would that give us a tool to work with? After all we are the sum total of our thoughts. We are where we are today because of the decisions we've made during our lives, and decisions are thoughts.

Remember I said the subconscious affects our behaviour? Well I want it to affect our behaviour in a positive not a negative way. If we can do that, then we are on the right track.

Firstly, I would like to explain how the mind was explained to me all those years ago.

The mind, the therapist told me, is essentially made up of two separate parts—the conscious and the subconscious. The conscious is the bit we all know about. It is the part that we all use day by day to think with and to receive with. We have little difficultly understanding the conscious mind. But behind this conscious mind lies the subconscious and for us adults there is a division between them. However when we are little children the division between our two minds is very indistinct and the younger we are the less effective that division is.

When we are young we are very 'impressionable' because most of the things we see hear and feel go straight into our subconscious. No barrier, no filter, no critical analysis, *straight in!* The trouble is that most of the information received by many youngsters is negative. "Poor little Johnny, he's very shy you know!" "Little Jane will never be a beauty like her sister!" and so on. We live in a negative world.

It isn't going to change.

Now the subconscious is a memory bank. It receives information and stores it. It can't tell the difference between past present and future. It can't tell the difference between truth and fiction. It can't tell whether the information it receives will be benign towards you or malignant. It just receives and remembers. As we grow up and mature we gain the ability to filter the information the subconscious receives but we are left with a load of rubbish in our subconscious that can affect our lives forever!

It stands to reason, therefore, that if we are going to effect change for the better we have to do a little housekeeping. We have to get rid of the rubbish.

Now that makes sense!

The trouble with many people is that they don't know how to open up the doorway to the subconscious. If you knew how to do that, you could, in some way clean up what is in there.

Well the good news is, *you can!* All you have to do is relax. Go to some quiet, peaceful corner where it is warm and safe. No interruptions, get comfortable, sit or lie down and consciously relax your body. Relax bit by bit. Start with the top of your head and work your way down the entire length of your body, talking to it and breathing easily and rhythmically. Let your whole body become a rag doll until all your muscles are soft and completely inactive. After a while you will discover that, not only has your body relaxed, *so has your mind.*

You are beginning to break down the barrier that exists between your conscious and subconscious and attain what is known as the *'alpha'* state. You are beginning to achieve the ability to do some house keeping. The subconscious cannot tell the difference between truth and fiction, past, present and future. It just receives impressions.

When I first tried this technique it was, as I have said, done to help me cure a stutter. I was trained to give my mind positive input. Simple phrases such as,

"I speak clearly"
"I speak fluently"
"I enjoy speaking"
"I find it very easy to speak in public"

"I enjoy it"

and so on.

I am not saying that I experienced an instant 'cure', it took time, but my stutter slowly began to improve. It wasn't cured in time for me to take pilot training, but over a period of time it went away. The only time it returns today is when I am asked to read aloud. I don't know why.

Over the years I have thought very carefully about this simple control one can have over the mind, and have become convinced that anyone can change their *attitude* if they have the desire to do so, all you have to do is unlock the door to your subconscious and then feed it with healthy food!

There is a saying, "Stand guard at the door of your mind!" which implies that if you don't, then your mind can't protect itself against rubbish and it is this rubbish that can cause your downfall!

Once I became convinced that I could change the contents of my subconscious, my life began to change. I began finding *solutions to problems* more easily and this had the effect of shrinking problems to their proper size, so that I saw them for what they were, *opportunities.* Opportunities to improve myself in such a way that I got much stronger and much more confident. I began to take control!

Positive Self-Talk.

We are where we are because of the way we think! If we don't like where we are and would prefer to be somewhere else, we had better change our thinking. Positive self-talk can help us do just that!

Now, before you go rushing around talking to yourself and causing concern to those around you, let's find out what self-talk is all about. We all do it you know, talk to ourselves, we just don't realise we are doing it. But when we say things like, "I'll never make it!" or "It's too late for me, I'm too old!" or "I bet I don't get this job." or "I'll never own a house like that, it will always be too expensive for me," we are indulging in self talk of a very dangerous and destructive kind. Remember we said that the subconscious cannot tell the difference between truth and fiction, past, present and future? Well, every time we make a statement, even to ourselves, we are building little memory banks in our brain which are going to affect our behaviour. We don't even have to say it out loud. It is enough to say, "I don't think I can do that!" and as sure as night follows day, it will have it's effect on our performance

What we have to do is change this negative thinking around and create a positive 'outlook'. How? By applying the same principles but in a *positive* way.

First, get to know your enemy. By that, I mean, you must start to acknowledge that you do indeed have some negative traits. Get yourself a piece of paper and draw a line down the middle, head the left hand side 'Negatives' and the right hand side 'Positives'.

Now on the left, start listing all those things about yourself that could be classed as negative. Let your mind run free! Don't think too much about each item; just let yourself indulge in a little 'brainstorming' of your own. Write as many as you can. Don't be concerned by the length, long or short, just be *honest*. This is for your benefit alone. This list is going to help you to improve your attitude, which in turn will improve your performance, which will go a long way to improving your bank balance!

When you have put down all the negatives you can think of stop, re-read the list and move over to the right hand side of the page. Next to each negative try to think of its opposite number, its positive. For every negative there is a positive.

I'm tempted to give you a list of negatives and positives, but have resisted the urge, because I don't want to put ideas in your head. Once the list is complete, look at all the positives you have accumulated, and thinking about them as a whole, start writing a statement of your *intent*, containing most, if not all the positives. A typical statement would go something like this...

*"I will **succeed** in my chosen field of.....................because I am entering this work with an **enthusiasm** that will grow each time I go to work. I am a **strong** salesperson because I plan and create the **activity** that is **positive** and **fulfilling**. I am **energetic** and get things done. People **enjoy** my company and I like people. The **high income** I earn is a direct result of **honest effort**, and I try at all times to give the best **service** that it is possible to give! I am the **best salesperson** I know. I **prospect continually**, **appoint easily**, **present professionally**, and **close strongly**. I will have $.......................in investments by (.............. date..............)!"*

Most of the positive words above (**in bold**) come from a real life list. *They are the positives!*

Don't take the easy way and just copy the one I have shown you here, even though it will work for you, it won't do the same job as *your own statement!* What you have to do now is make enough copies of this affirmation, so that you can put it in various places and this will help you to remember your statement. The bathroom mirror is a good place, as is the sun visor in your car and your wallet or purse. It needs to be somewhere where you can't miss it, and as soon as you see it, read it to yourself and read it as though you mean it. You want your subconscious to sit up and take notice and in that way it will slowly but surely begin affecting your *behaviour*.

You will start to notice that you are feeling more confident, more alive, and people will start to treat you differently too. A little more respect perhaps? A bit more attention? They will be interested in your opinion and seek your advice and this is because they have noticed a change in you. They seek your company because they feel you are enjoyable to be with and profitable to know.

It is not possible to over emphasise the importance of *spaced repetition* in the process of changing the way you think. It is after all, the way you got to be where you are now— repeated instructions—repeated images—repeated successes and failures have all gone into making you the person you are today. It took time, so take all the time you need to create change, be patient and you will see your behaviour change in such a way that you will become the person you want to be.

Life is not so much a question of getting, as a matter of becoming. Keep asking the question *"what am I becoming?"* The simple fact of the matter is, that if you can *become* what you want, you will *get* what you want!

In other words, don't try to change the world, change yourself! Work harder on yourself than any job you have and the job will be done well! It is what makes the difference to our lives, that inner strength, that calm, that confidence. It shines through in all the good and the bad times. It is your support. So take your positive affirmation and make it a part of you and realise that while you are doing that, you are writing your own future. Think of that—designing your own life! There *is* no better way!

Notice most of the statements made in the affirmation are in the present tense. You must be able to mentally put yourself in the picture. To see, feel, touch and taste your success. You must put on this new suit of clothes in such a way that it becomes yours.

The method I have shown you here works because you have taken the trouble to build your own positive statement, not relied on somebody else. The simple act of acknowledging your *own* negatives and changing them into positives makes your statement as unique as you are! The positive step you have taken towards housekeeping, (clearing out the rubbish) will lead you to a clearer understanding of how successful people think. If you can do that, guess what you will become. That's right successful!

Don't run away with the idea that this will be a permanent cure for all your ills. You must constantly stand guard at the door of your mind.

Some years ago the news has come through that Greg Norman had won his second British Open. This time at Sandwich, and I was interested to hear his remarks when asked what he had done to pull himself up from sixty-three in the world rankings to just three!

Greg Norman said, *"It started when I took a good look at myself in the mirror and asked what do I really want to do? Do I want to be the very best I can be? And the answer was 'yes'. I enjoy competition and have the competitive edge. In the round I have just finished, I did not play one bad shot, apart from one lapse on the green, (which turned out to be a good lesson anyway) all the shots I played were perfect! I am not a boastful person by nature but today I stand in awe of myself! When undesirable thoughts entered my mind, as they did from time to time, I concentrated on getting rid of them and replacing them with positive thoughts, and I succeeded!"*

If there was ever a greater endorsement of the power of positive thinking, I have never heard it. Talent alone won't do it. Greg Norman was down at number sixty-three and yet he had all the talent he needed. It was his *attitude* that needed polishing just as much as his technique!

The world is full of talented failures. I am sure you know some. Perhaps they are closer to home than you care to admit. What is talent, after all, but the ability to do things well? *We all have the ability to do things well!* Take any skill and work on it regularly, day after day, whether it be a musical instrument or playing tennis, or learning a language and in time anyone can become an expert.

Every top salesperson I know started out, naturally, at the bottom and learned the technique over time, to perfection. It is a learned process; you are not born with this or any other skill. *Anyone can gain skill.* And yet not everyone succeeds. Why is this so? Why are there a million talented failures in the world? Is it lack of confidence? Perhaps. Is it lack of money? No definitely not. Is it lack direction? Perhaps.

It all has to do with your attitude! The way you see things. The way you see yourself, other people, your job, your boss, your future. How much effort are you willing to put in to change your attitude? If it needs to change (and I would lay a bet it does) what are you prepared to do to change it? One of the million talented failures of the world will read these words, be mildly stirred by them and go back to being where they were. Or they could take up the challenge, do the work, follow the rules and forever change their way of life.

They will be one of those people that seem to shine. Stand

out in the crowd. Lead from the front. Show the way. People like this can show others that the future is in their hands and their hands alone. They can make their own futures so exciting that when they show it to others, people say, "Wow, is that your future? Where did you get it? It is terrific. I wish I had one just like that!" And you know, you can!

Just like Greg Norman the golfing champion, you too can look in the mirror and say "What do I really want to do?" and if the answer is "I want to be successful!" then you have taken the first step. You have realised that desire is an essential ingredient is developing a success attitude. I have never met a successful person yet who hasn't *wanted* to be successful. You don't get there by accident. You have to want it and you have to want it, badly! Don't wish it would happen. Make it happen. Dennis Waitley says, "Losers *let* it happen, winners *make* it happen!"

There is a promise I can make you even before you get there. *Succeeding is a lot easier than failing!* It is hard to fail! It's hard to *not* try! To sit around doing nothing. To have no goals, no desires, no wants. It is hard because failures have no money! They have placed themselves in a 'no win' situation that makes them poor. *Yes, placed themselves!* We are all self-made, and yet it is only the successful people that will admit it! Funny isn't it? Most of those people who have not made it are always blaming the other person. Never themselves. It is never their fault. 'I didn't get a good education.' 'No one would lend me the money to start,' and so on. My suggestion to the failures is to put yourself at the top of the list of reasons for not doing well. And when I say put yourself at the top, I mean put your *attitude* at the top. It is your attitude that is affecting your behaviour more than any other factor. Come on! We have all got problems; you are not the only one! It's how you *deal with* those problems that makes the difference. What are they but *opportunities?*

How do you get this outlook on life? By taking your statement and reading it to yourself regularly. Use 'spaced repetition' to help you absorb the good. Take in a little bit at a time, regularly. Like exercises for the body, the brain will continue to absorb and benefit from the positive input even after it has received it.

Try and imagine what life would be like if your attitude was positive and optimistic all the time; that every time you were met with a 'difficult' situation you were glad of another challenge. Glad because you would know that because you are who you are, nothing is going to stand in the way of your progress. It is all in the way you look at it! Next time you are faced with a problem, try finding the solution and you will discover that the problem was just another stepping stone to your success. Problems can be welcomed because they can show you the way.

Try this simple exercise. Next time you are faced with a situation that would normally annoy you, see it from a *different point of view!* See it with your new attitude. You may be in traffic for instance and some clown cuts in causing you to brake; pretty annoying eh? Enough to make anyone angry? But in this case remember *nobody can make you angry without your permission!* Where, after all, does your anger come from? Inside you! From *your* brain, and that is something that *you* control. It's not the traffic; the traffic doesn't care!

This other driver doesn't even know you! May not have even realised he *had* cut in and if he did realise, then it is a character revelation of a most unflattering kind. What has he done after all? Pushed in. It is no big deal. It isn't going to affect your journey one bit. Don't lose your cool. *He* won't even know will he? But *you* will! There is no point in getting angry on your own, now is there? Don't let him affect your attitude. It is *your* attitude to control, *your* way. By taking this kind of control you will do yourself no harm at all and might even turn out to be a better driver. Last but not least, think; have *you* never cut someone off?

Please don't misunderstand me I'm not talking about letting people walk all over you. I'm talking about you taking control of your reactions and emotions, so that you can be the kind of person you want to be. Save your energy for something much more important, *your journey to a better life.*

How to eliminate worry

How do you shape up in the worry department? There is no better profession than selling to create worry. What if *this* happens? What if *that* happens?

I used to be the world champion worrier. I would wake up in that dreadful hour at night, when all is dark, all is still, and I would lie there with nothing to think about but my worries, and boy don't they grow at night! I'd even worry about going back to sleep. Ever tried *that.* It's guaranteed to keep you awake all night! You get so tired you can't work properly and that causes more worry. I tell you, it's a vicious cycle!

So let me say this right up front. *Most of the things I have worried about in my life have never happened!* So I began to wonder what all the worry was for? It certainly didn't alter anything. It didn't prevent unpleasant things happening—it didn't cause anything to happen (except loss of sleep). It just sat there like a great big weight on my back serving no purpose. I began to wonder if I could get rid of this burden so I sat down to analyse what made up this thing called worry.

Take staying awake at night as an example. I decided to

say to myself in those dreaded morning hours. 'So I'm awake. So what? I'm still resting, I'm still healthy, sleep will come if I let it.' I would then relax, breath deeply and rhythmically and enjoy the sensation of the quiet, the calm and rest. 'It doesn't matter.' I would say 'It doesn't matter this is great!' I don't need to tell you, in no time at all, I was asleep! Simple? Of course. Most solutions are that simple.

What about worry about other things? Well first of all, there is no point in worrying about something over which you have no control. Quite obviously if you can't control events, then worrying is only a waste of your energy.

Supposing you have a sick friend. He is either going to improve or deteriorate and in either case you cannot control events. You would be much better off (and so would your friend) if you conserved your energy and thought of a way to help. Show concern, by all means, but worry, no thanks it is not productive.

What if you worry about business? And here is where I really object! Business *is* something you can alter, where you *do* have control and where, with your new found attitude, you can plan measures to improve your business and then *take action!* I promise you, with all that action going on you won't have time to worry!

Worry is for people who have time on their hands, people who don't have enough to do. Replace worry with *action* where you can, and *a positive attitude* where you have no control over events and you will see this thief of time and energy disappear. And when that happens you have much more energy, so that you can get on with the important business of making *you* successful.

Every day that goes by, you will be discovering more and more ways of using your new attitude to push you further forward, because you will automatically find those ways. You won't even have to consciously think about, your subconscious will do it for you. This powerful machine in your mind that no computer will ever be able to equal, will slowly take control of your positive, constructive activity and show you ways you never even thought existed to create for you *your* future and *your* happiness.

What is a success attitude?

What makes the difference between success and failure? Certainly not hard work by itself! I know plenty of hard working failures. People who go to work each day, put in a mighty effort, never shirk their duty and yet still can't pay the bills. So not only are they working hard, they are worrying themselves into an early grave. Most people lead lives of 'quiet desperation'. Never quite getting ahead, never quite being able to take that next step. That's *most people!*

Is it a fair question to ask, in that case, what do the successful people do? What makes the difference?

Firstly I believe that *successful people do the things that failures don't like to do. They* don't like to do them either by the way, *but they do them.* Remember we talked about desire? About wanting to? It has a lot to do with that. You see successful people would rather put up with the pain of doing it. Of going the extra mile so that they can *enjoy* being successful and failures would rather not put in today and have the dubious pleasure of 'taking it easy.' To avoid, if they can, the chance of failing in any effort they might put in, not realising that the *successful person has failed a number of times before succeeding!*

So *fear of failure* stops many people. Their attitude is one of 'it's no good trying that, it won't work and all my effort will be for nothing'. Rather than 'I am going to really put a massive effort into this program because, if it works, I will enjoy the fruits of success. If it doesn't work it will be a shame, but I will have learned something new, so that the next time I will have more experience to help me win. Either way I can't be worse off, and my *eventual success will make it all worthwhile!*

That is a success attitude. You can look at successful people and envy them if you want to, or you can join them. But understand that some of them failed many times before they succeeded. Some of them had to pick themselves up from disaster and start again. Why? Because they would rather be successful!

We are very lucky to be who we are. We can make choices, positive, intelligent choices; we are not cows or sheep. We are human beings and we can choose.

Which way will you go? Up or down? It really is *your* choice and yours alone to make, and once you make it you will discover that *success is easier than failure.*

You are unique in the animal kingdom in that you can make a *difference* in your own life. It is no good reaching the age of sixty-five and saying 'I've messed that one up, I'll have another go'. You can't go into rewind. What you can do is decide right now to design your own life. To take charge of your own future and make it happen!

How to overcome disappointments.

Many years ago when I was in my early twenties, I applied to a local TV station for the position of trainee cameraman. This was advertised as, 'no experience necessary, full training given' and so I thought here is my chance to get into an industry on the ground floor and learn the business from the start.

I duly turned up for the appointment and was rejected. I was very disappointed because I wanted to be a part of an exciting new industry.

Today as I look back, I thank my lucky stars I did not get that job. All the wonderful things that have happened to me since may not have happened if I had succeeded. Yet at the time I was shattered.

I wish I had known then what I know now! That is, that life is made up of failures and successes, disappointments and victories. Life is like that. It contains the good and the bad in varying proportions. Those proportions are probably just about equal and they are equal for everyone. *Not just you!* It isn't just *you* that is being dumped on. It's all of us. This is not going to change. We are dealt the cards at random and the deck contains good and bad. *It is what we do with them that makes the difference!*

Don't wish things were easier—wish you were better!

Make *yourself* better and life will improve for you.

Take disappointments for what they are, a part of living— an inevitable part. They will always be there, not just for you, but for all of us!

Self-pity will do nothing for you when you get a disappointment. If you doubt me take a census. Go around telling people how sorry you feel for yourself. Do they care? Do they show interest? Of course not, why should they?

Take your disappointment for what it is, part of the game. It will always be there, so learn to handle it in the only positive way there is, put it behind you and move on to better things.

It is all to do with your attitude. And your attitude is something *you* can control. The person that takes charge of his or her own thought processes is the person who has to win.

Always!

7.

Goals.

During the Vietnam War, both sides took prisoners. The Viet Cong took many Westerners as prisoners and in many ways the people from the Far East have an understanding of human thought processes that are unknown to us in the West. When a prisoner was taken, he was interrogated by his captors and questioned.

This was not the normal kind of questioning, name, rank, number, and so on. It was more along the lines of what did you do in civilian life? What do you plan to do after the war? What does the future hold for you?

The reason for all these questions was to discover if this person had any kind of view of his own life. Did he have any goals? How strong were they and how motivated was he about them?

Now you may wonder what purpose an enemy would have in asking all these seemingly irrelevant questions. Well they did have a purpose, and it was a good one. They knew that there were two kinds of people in the world, those with goals and those without. They also knew that those who were without, those who *let* things happen; those with no real purpose in life didn't need any tight security. They could be left in an open compound to wander about because the chances were they would not try to escape. However, those people who had a purpose in life. Those lucky few who had direction, energy, vision and ambition needed top security because it was these people who would try to escape!

What a lesson we can learn from this if we care to think about it and examine it. *People with goals are in control of their own destiny* and this applies as much if not more to the selling profession as anywhere else. We are salespeople right? Selling is a numbers game isn't it? The more we do, the more we approach, the more we present, the more we prospect the more we earn! Nothing I can think of lends itself more readily to the creation of goals.

When you have an occupation in which *the more you do the more you earn,* then you must have goals.

Many people in sales have income goals. They say they will earn a certain dollar amount this year and there is nothing particularly wrong with this. But I truly believe there is a better way. In selling we get paid for our activity. As we have already discussed, each different activity in sales can be costed providing we keep proper records of our earnings in relation to what we have done.

It would make sense, therefore, to have, as a part of our goal setting regime, activity goals. When one considers that a successful life is made up of a lot of successful *days* strung end on end, then it stands to reason that it would be of benefit to have daily activity goals. In other words, work out what it is you want to earn and then break it down into daily compartments, convert money into activity *and go for it!*

Now we are starting to design a future! Once we have got our daily activity requirements under control we must start thinking about our short, medium and long-term goals.

Short-term goals.
How short is short? One week? One Month? One Year?

Let's start with *right now,* this week. What is your education program like? Do you do any reading about your business? Use any self-improvement books or tapes, audio and video? Why not write yourself a comprehensive plan right now and follow through. Get up an hour earlier each day when things are quiet, and study. *It's a goal!* Write it down.

What is your record keeping like? A bit slip shod? Hit or miss? Why not decide right now to get organised. Starting right now keep a daily record of your activity and your business. *It's a goal!* Some of the greatest successes in the world have come from the smallest of decisions. What are your listening skills like? Why not make an effort to start listening to people with a view to understanding their wants and desires so you can help them? *It's a goal!*

One of the great answers to succeeding in selling is that you have to get the *bias* your way everyday! It doesn't have to be world shaking, it just has to be *your way* everyday! If you can do that, you will find that it is accumulative. It builds and builds in such a way that over time you find things going your way more and more. Your expectancy, therefore, is one of success, achievement and growth. Determine to get the bias your way all the time. *It's a goal.*

Are you a list maker? I am the worlds worst list maker but here *is* something you must make a list about; your short-term goals. Write them all down and keep them with you. Review them constantly and make sure you are improving all the time. Think of that positive bias and ensure it happens for you, every day. It is what successful people do!

Medium-term goals.

What is medium term? Six months? A year? Two years? It means different things to different people. What ever it means to you, you must follow the rules.

A goal has to be believable and attainable. Please don't get so carried away with the idea of your own success that you create unreachable goals. Unreachable goals are self-defeating because as you start to *not* reach them and slip further and further behind, you begin to loose heart and that causes loss of faith in yourself.

You have to be able to *creep up to* your goal. You have to be able to believe it, see it, touch it and live it. It must be *real* and in that way it will become a part of your psyche. If you believe it, really believe it, you will start to do the things that successful people do automatically! Not only that, you will find that although you are achieving more, it doesn't seem as though you are putting in any greater effort. In fact, you will find yourself enjoying life much more *because* you are an achiever. You are achieving your goal! There is no greater satisfaction than the achievement of your goals.

Some time ago we gave a beautiful silver salver suitably engraved as a prize for the salesperson of the year. Soon after the presentation one of our other salesmen came to me and asked what he would have to do to win this trophy next time. I told him and although it was more than he had ever produced before, I could see that he was excited by the thought of winning such a prize.

Over the following year we watched as this man pursued his goal. Each time I spoke to him he re-affirmed the fact that he was going to win that prize. I doubt he experienced a waking moment when the thought of winning left his mind. He probably even dreamed about it! Slowly and very surely we saw him improve and improve. His whole demeanour seemed to change. He was confident, cheerful and active. I don't have to tell you do I? He won the silver tray, and you know it wasn't really the tray he wanted, *it was the achievement of goal!* The satisfaction of knowing that he *could* do it. The feeling you get by being a winner.

Could he have done it without the silver tray? I don't know. What I do know is that he had not shown such determination before and in some way that trophy turned him on.

What will it take to turn you on? You have to find the key and it could just be in your medium-term goals.

Long-term goals.

It is the long-term goals that so many people don't consider. They are too far away and yes, it is true, they are a long way away, but too far? Never! You do have a future! Take my word for it unless something bad happens, you are going to get older. You'll be the same person you are now. Just older. So it is very important that you begin to set your long-term goals right now.

Recently I met an old friend who has just retired. This man has run a successful plumbing business for most of his working life, employing people and working on big projects. He has earned good money. He said to me "You know Rick, now I have retired I've realised I have a problem", "What's that?" I said. "Well I've suddenly realised I don't have sufficient money to retire in the way I want to." *Suddenly* realized? Wow! It takes the penny a long time to drop for some people! I remember this man telling me years ago that he was annoyed by all the salesmen who rang him in an effort to sell him a retirement plan and he never listened to one of them. He was too busy and not interested. Well he is not too busy now and he is certainly interested. *But it's too late!* You can't plan *for* the future *in* the future.

There has to be a better way!

Sit down and think about your long term goals *while you can!*

What about your children's education?

What about early retirement?

What about that holiday home?

What about that boat?

The list goes on. Want a world trip? It's yours! If you plan for it (and it is your *genuine* goal.)

Why not *you* tasting the wines of France with the warm sun on your back, as you sit in a vineyard just outside Bordeaux? Why not *you* trekking through the Himalayas looking at the crystal clear vistas? Why not *you* drinking in the atmosphere of the opera in Milan?

What ever it is, it can be yours. Not may be, *can* be—if you finally get yourself organised with some real goals.

Write Them Down.

It is vital to proper goal setting that you spend time writing down your goals. In this way you are transferring some of the responsibility to paper. The act of writing something down, in some way *confirms your intent.* It creates 'hard copy' which you can read over and over again. It gives a sound base from which to start operations and it allows you to adjust your goals and therefore your game plan, as you need to.

Goals that are not written have a tendency to become unimportant and float away into the ether, never to be seen again. Not much value in that!

Don't hesitate to adjust your goals. There are many reasons why your original goal is no longer accurate. We live in what is at best, an uncertain world in which changes take place. Inflation affects the value of the dollar in time and any dollar goal needs to be adjusted. Domestic circumstances can change, another reason for adjusting your goals. It could well be that you find you are already passing your goals expectation, so increase your goal. If you find yourself falling behind it might be an idea to re-adjust downward in order to make your goal more realistic.

Always keep your goals in sight and real. They are not *dreams* they are *goals.* There is a big difference we all have dreams of course and they are important. Take away our dreams and we begin to die. But dreams are not goals because they serve a different purpose. Dreams nourish us and help us develop and grow in stature. Dreams can protect us from some of life's harsher realities. Dreams allow us to escape sometimes, into a world of our own making.

Goals, on the other hand give us a purpose, a reason for action. They generate within us a desire to change the way we are and also give us the strength to effect that change.

Without well thought out intelligent goals we became inert. And the 'State of Inertia' is the worst place to be. When we are inert we have no *effect* on anything and the world around us can do whatever it will.

If you think about your life as I do about mine, then you will agree there has to a better way. Take charge of your future by aiming it at goals that will help you live the kind of life you really desire and you will be amazed at what you can achieve.

Given *enough reasons* we can achieve the most extraordinary things!

Another important piece of information for you, is that you won't achieve *all* your goals and the reason for that is that things happen that are outside your control. You mustn't let the bottom fall out of your world simply because you have been stopped from achieving something you wanted. Part of maturity, part of being an adult is to understand that sometimes, you lose. Now you might not like it. You might not even agree with it. But one thing is certain. You must *understand it*. You must have the basic understanding that occasionally things don't go the way you planned. It is not the end of the world! As long as you are still standing, moving, breathing then you *can* win.

It is when you are down, that your true inner strength shows through. That strength will come from, and can only come from *your* goals; the goals that *you* have set, the goals that *you* want. The goals that will motivate *you* so that your head rises above the rest and you become what you really want to be. A winner! A champion!

Thirteen Decisions to Success.

There comes a time in every successful person's life when he or she makes some decisions. Some do it very early in life and others leave it a lot longer. It is always best to do it earlier but *it is never too late!*

Many people I have spoken to have the urge to make decisions but lack the basic knowledge required to start the decision making process. I believe there are definite steps one must take to arrive at a series of correct decisions that lead you to a more successful future.

Before you start this process you are going to need some notepaper and you must have no interruptions.

Here, then are thirteen decisions you can make to help you go in the right direction.

1. Decide what it is you *enjoy!*

We do best that which we enjoy! You will never succeed at something you genuinely dislike. Oh, you will do it for a while, really have a good go at it, but you will *not* succeed. The world doesn't work that way. Why is it do you think, that some people like to do a certain thing whilst others hate it? Surely *that* is a signpost? It is part of a template that you can either fit into or not. These thirteen decisions will help you to discover *your* template.

Enjoyment is a natural part of life. It isn't *just* supposed to be there during your leisure hours! It can be with you most of the time. I'm sure you have noticed that when you doing something you enjoy, you have more energy, much more energy than you have when you are doing a chore that you don't enjoy, one of those jobs that you have been putting off day after day until it *has* to done!

Tasks you enjoy get done straight away and in many instances are done before they need to be! That is part of success!

2. Decide what it is you are *good at!*

This decision goes hand-in-hand with number one above. Have you ever noticed how people improve at the things they are good at? They work at it over and over and get better and better.

Little children who are naturally good at music progress not because they are told to, but because they just can't seem to help it. It is as though there is some inner driving force that almost makes them continue to practice, to work at it, to improve.

Same with sport, when we know we are good at a certain sport we do it more, and in the doing of it we improve and succeed. So decide right *now* what it is you are *good at*. It may not even be something that the 'world' would say is important, but if you are good at it, you will amaze yourself at how valuable it will become and we get paid for value!

3. Decide where you *want* to go!

You can't get there if you don't *want* to. I have never met a successful man or woman who hasn't wanted to get there! And when they are there they enjoy it. *Desire is one of the key fundamentals of success.* Without this all-important ingredient our 'success cake' won't rise.

Why do you want to be successful? Surely you can continue to live as you do today? Many people do. It is certainly less effort. You don't have to do anything do you?

Well the reason you should want to succeed is *desire.* If you want to badly enough you will get there. But first you must decide where it is you *want* to be. Sometimes people find this a little difficult to do. To these people, I would suggest making a list. Start writing down 'wants' as they come into your head, some of them may be incorrect or unrealistic, but just get your mind going on what it is you really want. Imagine yourself having it right now. Do you feel comfortable with it? Does it fit? Do you really want it, or do you just think you *should* want it because other people want it?

It is very important that this decision is the right decision and not something you think you *ought* to want. It has to fit you otherwise the chances are, it will not be a real goal.

Once you have decided what you want, dress it up! Make it real, put yourself in the picture. Touch it, see it, smell it, live it, *make it real!*

4. Decide *when* you want to get there!

You'll never get there soon enough without a *deadline.* Deadlines have a habit of *making* things happen. You must have reasonable destination parameters. We have all heard people say, 'One day I'll do this or that.' We have probably said something similar ourselves. The trouble with this is that 'one day' never seems to arrive. Why should it? *It hasn't even got a name!* You must identify that 'one day' so that it becomes *'the day'*. Be sensible about it and make that future time a *possible* time. We are not looking for miracles, what we require is a goal that can be achieved by doing, every day, those things that, when added up, will inevitably lead to our eventual success by *'that day'*.

5. Decide *why* you must get there!

Reasons always come first; *results* come next. There is not much point in striving to achieve something if the reasons for doing it are not valid. Think carefully about why you want the things you *think* you want because it is certain that if your so called desire does not, in the end, *have enough depth,* than your desire won't last! It's like a love affair!

We all do things for different reasons. Some people do things for other people, that's a good reason! The desire to make sure that someone benefits from what we do is an excellent reason to achieve. Some do things because other people say they will never do it. Now *that's* a good reason to achieve. Just proving them wrong can be satisfaction enough! Some people do things because of ego. It's a great reason! A healthy ego that drives you on, helping you to meet your own worthwhile goals, can only be good!

Some people do things because they are desperate. It's called *inspirational dissatisfaction.* "I'm not going to live like this any more!" It's a great reason!

Some people do things because the thought of living

life *without* having done it is almost unbearable. It's a great reason!

Whatever your reasons are make sure they are valid and make sure you *write them down* so that you can review them regularly.

6. Decide *what* you are going to do and *how* you are going to do it.

Positive mental attitude is fine and it gets you pointed in the right direction but there must come a time when you have to *do* something. That's right! It isn't going to happen just because you want it to. Don't let your goals become a 'wish list'. At some point you have to decide on a *plan of action* and when you have done that, cross out the word 'plan' and take *action*.

I have always found it very difficult to think in terms of large chunks of time. I can only get organised if I take reasonably small steps. So it may be of help, if you take the days you are given and make sure that you achieve a positive result every day. By that I mean determine what you have to do to achieve your eventual goals and then set your short-term goals to come in line with those longer aims. It all adds up to making sure your ship is going in the right direction and *going fast enough to get there on time*!

7. Decide what *activity* targets you are going to set yourself!

You are paid for your activity. Funny thing about selling as a career, you are not, in the end, paid for your results. What you are paid for is *the activity that leads to those results*!

So unless you make a concerted effort to work out your activity schedule, you won't really know where you are going will you? If you don't know what activity is needed for you to achieve your aims, ask. Never be afraid to ask someone who knows. Then try them out until you have figures of your own.

8. Decide what you are going *to do with it* when you have achieved it!

There is not much sense in achieving something unless you know what to do with it, when you have got it.

A friend of mine planned his life in such a way that he retired early. His aim was to stop work at forty-five years of age. Well he achieved his goal at forty, a spectacular effort, I'm sure you would agree. The only problem was, he didn't know what to do with his new found 'freedom.' He had never thought about the consequences, all he wanted to do was stop work. What then? He had never planned what to do with it when he had achieved it. He was driving his wife and himself and the rest of the family crazy. What did he do? He went back to work!

So make sure you know what you are going to do with your goal when you've got it and *don't hesitate to make some changes* if you feel it is not right.

9. Decide what price you *have* to pay. (Not what you are prepared to pay.)

There is a difference. I know that you *are* prepared to pay a price. You want to be successful, right? But what you are *prepared* to do and what you *have* to do could be two entirely different things.

By sitting down and carefully working out what will be required as the days, weeks, months and years go by, you will be able to come up with reality, and it *is* this reality that you have to come to terms with, if you are ever going to make your goal real!

10. Decide *if* you are prepared to pay the price!

Do you *want* to *succeed* badly enough? You can't dream your way to success.

When I talk to people who say they have set goals for themselves, I can very often tell if those goals are real to them. When I question them about their goals I get the impression that in some cases the goals are too vague. *That's a bad sign!* But worse than that, they don't quite know what they should be doing, how much they should be doing, and when. What really puts the nail in the coffin is when they don't even know *if* they are prepared to do it!

Other people leave you in no doubt, they know how much, when, why and if. They even know what to do to readjust.

Do you want to succeed badly enough? Are you prepared to pay the *real* price?

11. Decide whether the prize is worth the price—*for you!*

Failures are not prepared to pay the price. Remember? 'Successful people do the things that failures don't like to do?'

Well you must decide whether you really want to do it. For some people the price is too high and as long as they think that then, for them, it will never work.

You can't 'drift' up stream. You have to work at it. Now it is at this point, in your goal making procedure that you have to be completely honest with yourself. Are you prepared to pay the price? Whatever you have worked it out to be? Do you want success *so badly* that all the things you have to do to get there pale into insignificance beside the wonderful thrill of achieving all those things you have set for yourself? Unless you truly feel the prize is worth the effort, well I won't say it!

If, however, you look at the task ahead with all its difficulties, all its traps and pitfalls, with joy and excitement and not a little pride, then *go for it*. Because with that kind of attitude, you must succeed!

12. Decide how much you *want* to succeed!

It is in the *want* that the secret of your long-term success lies. Planning alone won't do it. Wishing won't and neither will talent. Luck won't do it, not even opportunity. Hard work by itself won't do it. Perhaps persistence comes close. But above them all is *desire. Burning desire*! And that must be coupled with the rest. It is the cement that binds it all together and keeps your energy at that high level all the time. Only the achievers of the world are blessed with that!

13. Decide to do it—or die!

Once you decide to do it. There is no going back. Economic death can be as bad as the real thing.

What I am about to say can apply to any developed nation.

I look around me and I see opportunity! It's everywhere! I'm sure if you looked at your surroundings with a fresh look, a new attitude *you* would see it too.

Opportunity is one of those commodities that has no limit, there is no ceiling, no lid. It has no boundaries. Opportunity only has horizons and the interesting thing about horizons is that you never reach them. They roll on ahead of you, beckoning you to go still further.

In a climate like that, you must be able to do it. Not just *decide* to do it, but *do it*! And you will find that in the doing of it, you will be creating your own source of energy that will lift you up and carry you forward to where you *plan* to be.

So decide now, right now, to do it!

Sharing Your Goals.

Should you tell other people about your goals? Of course! There is no point in hiding your future away. Just a word of warning however, share them with people who understand! People who are close to you and know how you think and won't put doubt in your mind.

A new goal is a very fragile thing it needs time to take root and start to grow, and sometimes a word in the wrong place can set this new goal back, can even kill it off. So guard it carefully, nurture it, defend it. That's why you must only let those people you trust get to see your goals. They will help it become strong and healthy. Eventually, it will be strong enough to survive anything. Strong enough, so that *it will even look after you!* At the start, however guard it against the natural negatives of the world.

Understanding success.

Success is the *'progressive realisation of your own worthwhile goal'.* That means that success must be a journey, not just a destination. You are being successful as long as you are on track, making adjustments as you go along, up or down, and constantly striving to beat your own standards. As long as you are doing the best you possibly can, then you will *become* the best you can possibly be. How do you know that you are doing your best, what measuring stick can we use to make sure that each day we are putting in our maximum effort?

First of all, people who are being successful just know!

They have the inner confidence that gives them the knowledge that they are, indeed, succeeding!

We certainly know when we are not performing at our best, because we all have that voice inside that, at the end of the day, tells us we should have, we could have, we didn't! We had time didn't we? We had opportunity didn't we? We had reasons didn't we? Perhaps what was missing was the *will*.

In the end it all comes down to one simple thing, *'to be a winner we have to have the will to win'*.

8.
Building A Business.

There must be thousands, if not hundreds of thousands of salespeople in the world who go out everyday and do a terrific job. They know selling inside out. Their techniques are flawless and their work habits immaculate. They are achieving regular and profitable results moving product, helping people enjoy services, expanding their territory and prospecting new markets all the time. These are the people who collect the trophies, win awards and receive the accolades of their fellow salespeople and managers. It all sounds great—and it is! Except for one thing! Are these top people *building a business*? By that I mean building for *themselves*? Sure, the company they are working for is certainly building a business that is why they are employing salespeople. The more they sell, the more the company makes and there is nothing wrong with that. What I'm talking about is the salesperson building a business. Not to the detriment of their company but to *compliment* the success of the company.

The day must surely come when the very people who have played a key roll in helping the company grow, can grow themselves. When they cease to sell, is there anything left for them? Can they look at their operation and say 'I built that'!

Ask yourself who are the clients buying from, you or the company? If the answer is the company, it may be time to ask, "Why is it so?" If the answer is they buy from you *despite* the company, then maybe you should be looking to the company to recognise your efforts in a different way. A more permanent way. A way that allows you to build a business without harming the company in any way.

I believe that good salespeople are fundamental to the success of most operations and sadly are not given the recognition that their contribution deserves. However, my purpose here is not to change the world of sales, but to show you how you can, despite your individual circumstances, build your own business in sales.

Salespeople are in a very fortunate position because in most cases the only connection the customer or client has with the supplier of the goods or service is the salesperson. It stands to reason, therefore, that the same salesperson has a wonderful opportunity to make that customer or client his own. Building a business means building a clientele and the start of this building process is keeping client records. I am constantly amazed, in talking to salespeople all over the world, that many of you allow the company to keep the only client records, mostly on computer, and these records are accessed by the salesperson when required. No no! That is *not* the way it should be done! Firstly you need different information from the company requirements. You are in the people businesses and as such you need 'people' information on top of 'client' information. Remember all prospects and all clients and all customers are people! They have the same wants, needs and requirements as most people and you need to know what they are. You can't remember it all. It must be written down and filed.

I have no way of knowing what field of selling you are in or thinking of going into, but I'll make a bet that your clients will have the ability to buy from you more than once, in fact they could probably buy from you many times.

If that is the case then you had better make sure that you look after them, nurture them and ensure they remember *you*! It quite possible for you to build a machine that will keep working away, silently in the background, for your benefit and that machine is your clientele. But before you put this machine to work, you have to understand *how* it works.

What is it, do you think, that people want from their supplier. Service? Yes. Honesty? Yes. Reliability? Yes. And they like the human friendly touch. They like the idea of knowing who they are dealing with. And they like to be made to feel important.

Many years ago I was an oil company representative and it was my job to call on local farmers and try to get them to change the brand of oil and petroleum products they used. These people would buy in bulk, many of them were wheat farmers and used great quantities of fuel, as hard as I tried I couldn't get them to change to my brand. I called on them regularly, had all the technical information at my fingertips and did a great job (I thought) in getting all the strong sales points across. But still no sales.

Now farmers are a conservative lot and I soon discovered that I was facing an almost impossible task. Day after day I went out to fight my way through the farmyard dogs to try to talk the farmer into changing. The problem was they saw me as a 'company' man.

As the weeks and months went by and I thought more and more about this problem, I began to do something I should have done much earlier. I began to ask more questions! It didn't take me long to realise that there was a third force in the arrangement that I hadn't counted on. The local agent!

I discovered that the farmers did not buy from a company! In fact, in many cases they knew little or nothing about the oil company that supplied them. They dealt with the local agent. *Here was the salesman!*

When I analysed the answers I received from my questioning process, it was clear that each and every one of them thought very highly of this man and almost all of them considered themselves to be his most important customer. What a lesson that was! Not only that, they had been dealing with him for a long time and said that many times he had helped them out in a crisis and had even carried them over hard financial times. He knew them and their families well, and was something of a local identity.

One man told me that once, the agent had run out of a particular product that he needed and rather than hold him up, the agent had asked his opposition in town to deliver the required product to him—that's confidence!

I don't know if this local agent had ever had any sales training or read any books on how to win friends, but he certainly ran rings round me.

I began to realise even way back then that anyone can get and secure a good clientele simply by treating them as you would wish to be treated. Make your clients' problems, your problems. Make sure you always behave in such a way that it can never be said of you 'he's only interested in himself'. That is a loser's attitude.

As you develop your business in selling make sure that every new customer has the chance of becoming a long-term client. Keep in touch. To do this you are going to need as much information as necessary to allow you to do just that and keep this information on your computer. Many software programs are designed to retain the kind of information you require and to bring up that information when needed. Make sure you spend some time each week bringing your records up to date and ensuring that your clients are looked after.

Some of you may be saying 'but they are not my clients they are my company's' and my reply would be that they will never be yours if you don't do something about it. What have you got to lose?

One big car dealer recently sent a representative to a car dealers' seminar. They came back with this groundbreaking idea. Contact all the people who have bought from you in the last five years! Wow! You don't have to go to a seminar to learn this valuable information. You can apply it right now. Don't wait for your company to make a move. *You* do it and your enterprise will be reflected in your bank balance. Treat your job as though it was your business and it will grow and flourish until one day you will be able to call yourself a businessman! You want to be in charge don't you? In control? Of course you do, and that means it is up to you. Don't wait to be told, you're not a trained seal, do it *before* you are told and you will always be in demand.

If you are fortunate to be running your own affairs in business, make sure you are doing just that. Running your own affairs. When you are in charge of your own agency or company then you have a responsibility to look after your own clients because if *you* don't take on the job, then the opposition is just waiting to do it for you.

It's the person that gives service that wins. Take every opportunity to seek out people who need service and offer it. Find out from people what they expect. Ask questions. Starting today begin building a profile of a satisfied client in *your business.* If you were *your* client what would you want? Are you prepared to give it?

I have owned a number of houses during my life and each time. I have sold and bought through somebody different. It isn't as though these people went out of business, they didn't, it is just that they didn't see me as a long-term client. As soon as the deal was done you couldn't see these people for dust, they disappeared faster then a block of ice on a hot day, never to return. How sad! If only they had thought of keeping in touch, keeping me up to date and making sure that, should my situation change, I understood they would stand ready to help. Wanted to help. Wanted my business because I was important! Sad to say it is the same with all the car salesmen I have done business with over the years.

I know you might not win them all but you will get the *bias* on your side, and if you do that regularly you will inevitably start climbing that wonderful stairway to success. You will become a businessman who is in control of his own business whether you are self employed or employed it is all the same. You get paid for *value!*

I know a life insurance agent who has been in business for twenty years which means that he should have by now, had twenty years experience. Only he hasn't! This man has not kept personal records of clients and has to start from scratch every January. Far from having twenty years experience, this man has had one year's experience twenty times!

It is a tragedy that salespeople take so long to see the value in their own clients. They are so hyped up about making the next sale, they forget to build for the future. By showing a little patience and maturity they would discover, over the years, that they can secure a future for *themselves* by making their clients their own!

It doesn't happen overnight of course, but it does happen! Slowly but surely you will find business getting easier, prospecting becoming a natural part of your daily function and many times clients will be ringing *you* to buy more. People like to deal with those they trust and can rely on.

Why should they go out of their way to talk to strangers when you have proven to be of value to them?

To make this long term servicing commitment work for you, you have to be of value right from the start. You have to 'go out of your way' to do things that the average salesperson either won't or can't do.

What are some of these things that we can do to make our clientele remember us and value us? I have listed 10 ways here to help you get started and to keep you going.

1. Birthday Cards.

Sounds a bit corny? Don't you believe it! People don't really get many birthday cards; it is important to us isn't it? So make sure your clients receive a card from you on their birthday. Not a preprinted company card, but a personal card from you.

The first life insurance policy I bought was from a man called Ces Thomkins over thirty years ago and the reason I can remember his name is that for a number of years he sent me a card.

2. Christmas Cards.

Here you may be competing with a lot of other cards, but it is still worth it. It takes so little effort and can mean so much.

3. Passing on Information.

Many times you will be in receipt of information that

would be of benefit to some or all of your clients. A short note informing them is another way to keep in touch. Examples such as updated models, new services and price changes may all be of interest.

4. Giving Extra Services.

Many times the sales person is in a position to give extra service. It may be that a particular client is interested in antiques and you notice an article that could be of interest. Why not mail it to him or her with a short note saying you thought this would be of interest. If you think about it carefully there are many occasions when you will be able to be of extra service to your client. Of course you have to know your client details to do this. So keep records and keep them up to date!

5. Giving to Receive.

When was the last time a salesperson did something for you that he didn't really have to do? Not recently I bet? Not ever perhaps? If they did, it would certainly have a positive impact.

A friend of mine is a great referred lead getter and whenever those leads turn into business, he sends the nominator and spouse to dinner at a little Italian restaurant in his area. (By the way the owner of the restaurant is a client also.) When the people arrive they are shown to a reserved table and treated like very special guests and when that complimentary bottle of wine arrives they see the label has been printed to say, "Thank you for helping me build my business!" and is signed by the salesperson. That is what I call building a business!

Another salesman friend of mine holds an annual barbecue at his home for his special clients. It works wonders and always results in more business. Never be afraid to spend some dollars on your business. It's an *investment!*

6. Annual Reviews.

Perhaps your business lends itself to sitting down with your client on a yearly basis to discuss the latest trends in your business. He may need to alter what he is doing at the moment and even purchase more of whatever it is you sell. Always take notes at these meetings and file them away for future reference. A lot of new business is written as a direct result of annual reviews. You can do something that the company cannot do. Get face to face with your client so that he realises you genuinely want to help, and don't forget, this is another great prospecting opportunity.

7. Letting the client know you want to help.

So many people miss this vital step. Unless the client knows you stand ready to help him at anytime, you will miss out on the opportunity of doing just that. No client will ring you if he feels he is not wanted or appreciated. Tell him that you appreciate his business and are always ready to help him in the future. **"I'm only a phone call away!"** Don't forget other people are trying to make him their client too!

8. Getting people in touch.

There are situations where one client could help another. As an example a client may have a child who wants to learn a musical instrument and one of your clients is a music teacher. Get them in touch! It builds a strong clientele! One client may have the ability to arrange finance and another may need his services. Get them in touch! You can become very important to people as the person who can help solve problems. It is what top business people do. You have to know your clients well to do this.

9. Show appreciation.

A little while ago a friend of mine was in the process of buying a new car, so I suggested he get in touch with the person I had dealt with only a few months previously.

I rang the salesman and told him to expect a call from my friend and in due course he did.

No sale resulted from this introduction. You win some and you lose some. But I never heard from the salesman again! The least he could have done was ring me and thank me, first of all for thinking of him, and second for the introduction. Not a word! Some salesman! The lesson is, always show appreciation and you will always be a winner!

10. Go The Extra Mile.

Do more than is expected of you at all times. If a client needs to pick something up from a supplier and is too busy, why not offer to do it for him? People don't expect service and it's nice to surprise them. You will never lose by going the extra mile, putting in that extra effort. It is so easy at the time and always puts the *bias* your way. Clients give leads to salespeople who help!

Your client file, your business!

In many ways it is your client file that constitutes your business. It is worth a lot of money. It can support you in good times and bad. It is always there to lean on for support. When business gets a little slow and you feel like the whole world has learned the word 'no', turn to your client file and you will find new sources of inspiration. These are people that know you, trust you, have dealt with you. These people are still prospects as well as clients and even more importantly they know other people that you haven't met yet, and by applying the proven sales techniques you have learned, you can increase the size of your client file.

In servicing your clients you are in effect, *building a fence around your clients* and this fence prevents your opposition form breaking in. Your opposition's job is to get to your clients and sell them *their* services and if you allow this process to take place, you will find your business, rather than growing, is shrinking. All the work you have put in selling these people in the first place can be undone by lack of service. Don't blame your opposition. Blame your lack of service.

If you forget your clients, they will forget you!

I know many good face-to-face salespeople who love the thrill of the chase, the excitement of closing another sale and the prospect of earning very high income from making those sales, but they can't or won't service. They don't 'like' to do the 'boring' work needed to keep in touch with the people they have sold. Little do they realise that the people they have sold will never become clients until they have taken the trouble to build up a business relationship that will stand the test of time. We have to realise that the sales we are making today are more than likely with people who should have been some other salesperson's client. But that salesperson couldn't be bothered putting in the work.

If you are seriously going to make selling your lifetime career, and I sincerely hope you do, don't make the same mistake!

The 'M' Factor.

Some years back I was introduced to the 'M' Factor. The

'M' stands for marketing. I was in the middle of a slump with not many prospects, not many appointments and not a great deal of enthusiasm. I decided to talk to one of the more successful salespeople in our organisation and invited him to lunch. Incidentally, if you ever need some good advise, take a successful person to lunch. Now it's no good saying 'why should I take this person to lunch, he or she has got more money than me'. The investment of a few dollars on a meal could give you an idea that might change your life.

The person I took to lunch was very successful and appeared to have achieved all the things I was hoping for in my life. When I asked him where I was going wrong, he told me I was asking the wrong question. What I should be trying to discover he said, was *what should I be doing right.* So he asked me "Rick, what do you think you should be doing to improve your business?" I stared at him blankly. This is precisely what I had hoped *he* was going to tell *me.* Like all good salespeople he started by asking questions. "How many clients have you got?" I did a quick mental calculation and came up with about one hundred and fifty. He stared at me, this time with a look of surprise and said, "Then what is your problem?" I told him that I was in the middle of my third blank week, and could see no light at the end of the tunnel. "Obviously" he said "No one has told you about the 'M' factor?". "The what factor?" I replied.

"I want you to start writing down the names of clients." he said "But not just ordinary clients. These clients are slightly different. They are the people with whom you get on especially well. They are the people who you wouldn't hesitate to help and who you feel, would help you in return. When you have carefully sifted through the names of your clients, I want you to find fifteen that fit that description." I thanked my lucky stars that I had kept a detail of all my clients and could bring them to mind when needed.

The next day I met with my friend with my list of fifteen.

"Okay, now this is what I want you to do. I want you to ring these people and say "Peter, I am ringing you because I need your help and I knew that if I asked you for help you would give it. Is that okay?

And you make an appointment in the usual way. Now, when you meet these clients your objective is to get ten referred-leads from each of them right?"

"Okay." I said "But why would these leads by any different from others?"

"Because of the 'M' factor."

"I don't understand." I said,

"Have you ever noticed," he said, "That many times the leads that people give you are very much like the people themselves?"

"Well, yes." I said.

"And I asked you to pick out clients that you would help and who would help you in return?"

"Yes."

"Then they are *your* kind of people aren't they? And the chances are their leads will be your kind of people too. They will be *your natural market.* They will have the 'M' factor! Surely that must mean they will be easier for you to sell to!"

Suddenly I saw the light. It was so simple. Some people were easier for me to sell than others. We were on a common wavelength. Have you ever noticed that you click with some people more than others? You seem to get on much better, more relaxed? We all have this 'M' Factor going for us and we must utilise it in selling as much as we can.

Needless to say the one hundred and fifty referred leads I achieved from this simple exercise lifted me out of my slump and got me well and truly back on track. It was made possible because I asked someone who knew more than I did and I had *kept my client file up to date.* I shudder to think what would have happened if I hadn't taken the trouble to record the details of all my clients. Now I knew they were worth gold! So if you haven't yet done so, start keeping all the details you need about the people you sell to. Your future could depend on it!

Far be it for me to suggest salespeople change companies and suppliers from time to time, but we all know they do. How sensible it is then, to take with you wherever you go, your own client information file. If you don't take action on this simple task, you won't ever be a top salesperson who can command his own level of income and who will always be in demand. Don't leave it all up to the company. They are naturally doing business for their reasons, not yours. Take charge and make sure you always have somewhere to go and *someone* to talk to! Make sure that your clients always know where *they* can contact *you.*

We have all heard stories of a client buying from the opposition simply because the original contact had moved elsewhere. Make sure that you are always contactable by letting clients know your new location.

Map your clients.

A good friend of mine and a top salesman maps all his clients and contacts. He keeps a detail of everyone in his street directory and in that way he is able to call on important people when he is in the area. He tells me it is really amazing how much business and how many leads he gets simply by calling in when he is in the area. Make your clients feel that they are important to you and they will be!

This salesman always keeps a note of who he has called on, when and what resulted, so that before he walks in he can refresh his memory about the client or centre of influence. I'm not surprised that he is the top man in his field, he deserves it!

Talking about deserve it, you get what you deserve in selling, always! It never changes, if you put in, you get out and you succeed or fail because of *you.*

Most people like to deal with successful people, and if they see you as successful, don't be surprised if they ask to deal with you.

Funny thing about selling as a career. It gets easier the longer you are in it. You get to be *busier* but it gets easier. Over a period of time you will find that more and more of the things you do, work! And as you go through your day, providing you apply the principles of successful selling, you come to *expect* the best. The best from yourself, from your clients and from your prospects.

You expect the best from you plans as well, and so you should, the world is designed for success. Providing all the conditions are right, you can't help but be successful. So build your business brick by brick, client by client, because each client you get is as tangible an asset as any other asset you might build during your life!

9.
Success — What Is It?

What a word; 'success'. So many people have tried to define it and even more have tried to achieve it. Some have got there, most haven't! I have even met people who have got there by sheer accident and haven't realised it.

I wonder if success is a destination? I wonder if we can look into the future and see something, some indefinable thing that is waiting for us there in the future. When all our problems will be solved and we can sit back and serenely look at the view, breath the fresh air, and at last, do all the things we want to do. Whatever they are.

Does such a place exist? Perhaps, but mainly in our dreams.

But wait a moment, what are dreams and can they become real? And if they can, how can they?

I believe it all depends on how realistic these dreams of ours are. If you were born outside the USA and dreamed of becoming president one day, well, no I'm afraid not, they won't let you! You have to be born in the States. So cross *that* one off your list if you were born somewhere else. But what if you *where* born in the USA? Yes, it's achievable.

So dreams have to be realistic, attainable, achievable and understandable.

I wonder if success always has to do with money? Many

people think so. And for them it has a good fit. If it's what you want then there is nothing wrong with that. Money *is* important. I know this much, being dirt poor is no fun at all. I've been there!

I want you to think about someone you know who is successful. Somebody who has achieved all the things you think you want. Put them in your minds eye and see them going about their day-to-day tasks. Do you think they are happy? When you see this person or think about them is the predominant feeling you get from them one of contentment, of happiness? If you do then I believe this person is successful. Now that has to give us a clue to understanding success.

Take the case of Howard Hughes. On the outside he was successful, at one time he was the richest man in the country. He had a great career, he was famous, and he had many beautiful women, lots of money and talent to spare. Why then, did he end up a lonely, sick old man with no friends and only bodyguards for company? Could it have something to do with our idea of success not being what we think it is? Perhaps all the things he achieved didn't make him happy. In the end his billions went to six or seven cousins who hardly knew him. What is the ingredient that's missing in this man's life to make it complete?

In another part of this book you will read about goals and how to achieve them and I believe goals have a major part to play in whether we are successful or not. Goals can form a natural part of our daily life if we allow them. It's a sad reflection that so few people, and I include people who desperately want to be successful, have goals!

Are they *that* afraid of failing, they won't aim at a target to make them do the things that failures don't like to do? Goals are a part of being successful! If you don't have goals, all you have are wishes and most wishes don't come true. How many times have you heard someone say, 'I'd love to play the piano like that.' Oh yes, really? You have to actually *do* something!

Could it be that success means different things to different people? We know people are different from one another, have different personalities, different needs and desires. They even have different ways of thinking. Perhaps we shouldn't be dogmatic about success. The very things *we* see as signs of success could very well be the complete opposite in another person's thinking. So success isn't a fixed object, it can change from person to person and from time to time. As our situation changes it's quite possible our desires will change. We all grow and mature with time; our environment changes as do the people around us. Our ideas of success *must* change with time. *Because we change!*

OK let's take breath here and try to do a bit of creative thinking. If our idea of success is going to change with time and circumstance, what's the point of setting out on some path *now* which may lead us to somewhere we don't want to go? Good point! This is because we haven't yet worked out what success really is! What it means to us, what it will do for us, and why do we crave it so badly.

Many of us look at people whom we are told are successful and believe that if we were there we too would be happy. There, I've used a word happy and this word should form a very important ingredient in our definition of success. Can you be successful if you are not happy? How many so-called successful celebrities are unhappy? Judging by the number of stories we hear about drugs and failed relationships, not many! So are they successful? I don't believe so. What they thought would make them successful failed to do so.

Wayne Dyer says, 'Happiness is the key.' When I first heard this, I felt it was too simple to mean a great deal and yet it a strange way I couldn't get the phrase out of my mind. 'Happiness is the key.' I hope it will get under your skin too, just as it did mine. Of course it makes sense. All the positive things we do make us happy or will make us happy in the future. If you are not happy, change what you are doing and find something that makes you happy. The end result of 'being successful' should make us happy; if it doesn't then we are not successful. Oh, sure, in the eyes of others we appear to have achieved some success, but happiness comes from within, not from other people. Happiness comes from all the different things that have happened to us, all those events that have contributed to our understanding of ourselves as human beings.

The human race is designed for happiness. The fact that so many people are unhappy merely means they haven't yet found success. To them I say, 'It's not too late. If you are unhappy with your life today, change your life!' Life is too precious to waste on unhappiness.

To be happy is to be successful.

I don't pretend to know it all, but I do know this and I have said this before in this book. Success is the progressive realization of our own worthwhile goals. It is a journey, not a destination.

As we go through life, whether we like it or not, we have a roadmap stretching out before us. We can choose to take this path or that; it's up to us.

What we must do is choose the path we believe will make us happy, and if we make a mistake, *correct it quickly*. Don't waste time being unhappy, because 'happiness is the key!'

10.
What's it all about?

So what is this business of selling, and why is it so good for some and can be a disaster for others?

I believe there are four major items that go into making a great salesperson, **belief, desire, product knowledge and action!** None of these is more important than the other, but if any one is missing, then your efforts won't work.

Why is **belief** so important? It all sounds a bit evangelistic. Can't I sell if I don't believe? If my techniques are good enough and I close strongly enough then surely I will succeed? After all, the buyer buys the presentation doesn't he? Yes he does, and most people can see through a 'phoney' presentation. And by phoney I mean insincere, not from the heart, *you don't mean it!* They can tell by the way you talk, move and look at them and by your unconscious sign language.

We humans have had millions of years communicating with each other and we can tell when someone doesn't mean it.

The first thing to believe in is *yourself,* your skills, your confidence, your knowledge, your appearance and your experience. A tall order I grant you. But with time you can build a self image that reflects your belief.

If everything you do is done to the best of your ability you have nothing to be ashamed of. We have powers that can overcome all kinds of obstacles and a series of successes does wonders for the ego. It stands to reason, therefore, that if we take the time and effort to improve our skills and techniques then our self image is bound to improve. Drill for skill, get better and better at what you do, become the expert and your belief becomes unshakeable.

Then of course there is your belief in the product you are selling. Do you really belief it will help your prospect? Don't get hung up on the idea of whether it the best on the market. That is something too subjective, and depends on so many factors. No, what you should be concerned with is, will it do the job for this prospect?

If you can't truly believe in the product then in the long run you won't succeed at selling it. Oh, you might fool some people some of the time, but you will never have that sparkle, that brilliance, that flair and long term commitment that comes from talking to people about a product or service in which you **truly** believe! Belief is the foundation of your career as a sales person.

What about desire?

How badly do you want to succeed? Is it just a 'want to' or does it consume most of your waking hours?

Some people just drag themselves through life doing just enough to 'pay the lousy bills', and others seem to have an inner glow. They create an excitement around them that is almost tangible. People want to be with them as though this feeling is going to rub off on them. We have all met people like this and wondered what it is that makes them tick. I believe it is the desire in them that shows through like a light. It makes them glow. What is it that people say? Burning with desire? How true. You have to have a **burning desire!**

You can't get to be successful by accident. Everything has

to be right. Right for you and right for those around you. *And you control that!* That's right! You can be in control!

Now we come to product knowledge.

Have you ever been in a selling situation as a prospect, asked what you think is a simple question, only to discover the salesperson didn't know the answer? Shakes your confidence right? Particularly your confidence in the product. Why should you believe anything else this person is saying to you if they don't know *all the facts?* That's right 'all the facts'.

You have no right to be let loose on the unsuspecting public if your product knowledge is wanting. They deserve better!

The funny thing about product knowledge though, is that in real life you never have to use all of it. But you must know it. It's your product, and you never know when you are going to be asked a question. Not only that, what right does anybody have selling something that they don't know **all** about?!

So take the trouble to find out what makes your product or service tick. Read up on it. Study it. It is all part of your business. Your success!

Taking action!

When it comes to **action** you had better make it big! If you are going to take action, make sure it is *massive* action! It is action that makes the difference. The man listened to all the motivating tapes, read all the improvement books, learned all about the product and had faultless techniques. The only trouble was *he never left the house!*

When *you* contemplate taking action, stop contemplating and do it! Until *you* do it, it won't get done. You can't *think* it into being. Remember we said you get paid for your *activity?*

It's the only thing you do get paid for! There is no such thing as appearance money for salespeople. You have to actually perform. Take action! And make it massive!

Think of the fun you can have!

When I first went into selling, I found something I didn't expect. I was beginning to get a better understanding of people and the way they behave. I suppose I hadn't taken much notice of other people's behaviour before. It didn't seem important. I had been a lazy observer.

Now, as a salesman, I found myself watching more intently and noticing little signs that used to pass me by. Used to be unimportant. The more sales interviews I had, the more I found I could *read* people. I was beginning to see buying signals as well as signals of disinterest. "How interesting," I thought "People communicate in so many different ways!"

I hadn't noticed before, but the range of human language is almost limitless. I was also learning that by placing words in their right place, by using more or less emphasis at certain times I was having more or less effect.

Slowly I began to understand selling, and what it meant. It was powerful! I was able to get people to do things that only moments before, they weren't even thinking about. I could actually change people's thinking! Encourage them, persuade them, enthuse them, motivate them and get them to take action! And all this by watching people's reactions and using this knowledge gained by experience to *vary* my own presentation and get results. That's selling!

How interesting people are and what fun. It's the kind of thing that makes this profession of selling constantly filled with interest.

It's a people business, not a 'thing' business! The next time you are talking to someone, make the effort to note their reactions. How interested are they? What signs are they giving you that show you they are happy, sad, angry, bored or enthusiastic. Watch and learn. Become a student of people's behaviour. It will pay you so much in the years ahead because a salesperson has to be selfless.

By that I mean all the attention must be on the *other person!* Don't let your ego get in the way!

We all have, or should have, a healthy ego, but keep it in the background. None of us enjoy talking with the egomaniac. The person whose main topic of conversation is himself. When you are selling, you are a conduit, a vehicle, a channel. Through you, the benefits of your product must come through. If they don't, if *you* get in the way, you will never be a great salesperson!

So learn to give all your attention to your prospect. Concentrate on him or her with all your faculties and to do that, *you must know your presentation.*

Another thing I noticed was that many people didn't quite say what they meant. Things like "I want to think about it". When I knew that was the *last* thing they were going to do. They had given me too many buying signals along the way to mean 'no'. I discovered that very few people said "Rick, no thanks. I don't want it ". Once in a while someone said 'no', but not that often. Now if they didn't say 'no', they obviously wanted it and just needed pushing over the edge. I had to close. Thank goodness I learned *that* early in my career!

I used to read books with all the tricky answers to objections, and I would practice them. All I succeeded in doing was to *confront* the prospect, and that isn't selling. I had to learn how to sell the benefits of my service and that is all I have ever sold since.

Now you can't sell the benefits if you don't know what the

prospect *sees* as a benefit, and the only way you are going to find that out is if you ask questions, and plenty of them.

Years ago we were living in the country, and we were visited by an old friend, Brian Looker. In order to show him around, I took him to meet some of the people my company dealt with in the area. As I introduced him to all these people, farmers, businessmen, executives, I noticed he kept asking them questions. Questions about themselves and they really opened up to him! In two days Brian found out more about these people than I had in the two years I had been dealing with them. And they thought he was terrific. Long after he had returned home people kept asking me how he was getting on and when he was coming back. They thought he was great! It goes without saying Brian is a salesman!

What a lesson I learned. People love to talk about themselves! One of the most interesting questions you can ask of anybody is, "How did you get started in this line of work?" Boy, some of them can talk for hours! All you have to do is listen and they will tell *you* how you can sell them. But you have to listen carefully.

I believe that every time you have a sales interview, you make profit, whether you make the sale or not. You always profit by the experience, but only if you become a student. Be determined to learn from every interview. Take notes and study them, and after a while you will discover that you are handling difficult situations with greater skill. I takes time, but it's worth it.

As I progressed along this fairly steep learning curve, I noticed something else. In an interview it is easy to tense up, to become anxious and believe me it shows. If the prospect thinks you are tense, he tenses up as well. Are you telling the truth? Have you got all the facts? Are you leaving anything out?

I started to relax. Whenever I began to get a little edgy I would take a deep breath, sit back and relax. Since then I've been a great believer in *relaxed selling*. You know the prospect will, more often than not, reflect your mood. You relax, they relax, and relaxed people buy! Now whenever I notice things getting a little on the tight side, I just relax. Try it.

Learning to handle knock-backs!

One thing more than any other discourages people from coming into or staying in selling as a profession, and that one thing is being 'knocked-back'. Whether it is on the 'phone making an appointment, before the presentation, during the presentation or after, it is all the same. None of us enjoy being told 'no'!

The first thing to understand about our reaction to the word 'no', is that disappointment is perfectly natural. We, all of us, enjoy a 'yes' much more. A 'yes' is an agreement. It's what we are looking for. It is what selling is designed to do, get 'yes's.

But we live on planet earth, and on this planet there is no such place as 'Yes' Land'. That beautiful land we see in our dreams where everyone agrees with our point of view and does what we want them to do! If it does exist, then I for one have never found it.

If there were such a world in selling then *we* wouldn't be needed. There would be no need for salespeople because there would be no objections, no refusals and no *no's*. So thank you very much for all the no's, they keep me in a job.

Now I'm not saying that you should actually enjoy the no's, but you have to put them in their right place. They are, as we have said before, a part of the system, and they are *inevitable*. They are *going* to happen, they *must* happen, they *will* happen and we have got to get used to them.

It is our job to keep the no's down to a minimum. It is also our job to winkle out the 'false' no's. These are the no's that are not no's at all, but yes's in disguise, requests for more information on which to base a buying decision.

All this and more we have to understand if we are to succeed in selling. Just as there is no land where there are no no's, there is also no land where there are no yes's. Those yes's are out there alright and with a plan, a good solid work plan and persistence *you* will find those yes's. There are people out there right now buying your product from somebody, so you must always 'expose yourself' to the 'danger' of getting that yes. Persistence and determination will do it for you.

So is there anything good about the no's? Well for one thing they bring you closer to a yes that's for sure. For another thing they certainly make you a better salesperson. Why? Because you are always learning, and you learn as much, if not more, from the no's you receive as you do from all the yes's in the world. Let's face it, most of the yes's are easy! They are good for our ego, certainly, but they don't provide much of a learning experience. It is the no's that do that if, and only if, we are prepared to listen. Listen to our prospect and listen to ourselves. Listen and take notes. What happened? Is there anything I could have done to change things around? Was a sale possible? Did I miss something? Was there any part of the sales presentation where I felt I *had* made the sale, and did I perhaps lose it somewhere?

I'm not saying you should tear yourself apart, but you have to analyse. As time goes by you will find that your experience in dealing with people is getting greater and greater and one day you will wake up to find your confidence high, strong and *unbeatable!* So take the no's for what they really are *signposts to success!*

If you are in selling or thinking of going into the profession, I envy you. You have, or will have the most exciting and rewarding occupation in the world. The entire world of commerce depends on you. This is not to say that those people outside the selling sphere aren't important, of course they are. Products and systems have to be designed and administrators have to keep us all on the right track. Accountants have to make sure we make a profit and keep track of the money. But when it comes to excitement, freedom, job satisfaction, reward, innovation and earning ability, the profession of selling has it all. I have been selling for over thirty-five years and although there have been setbacks and disappointments; the many times when I have experienced success have outweighed any negatives. Not just outweighed those negatives but obliterated them!

Success is the only thing to remember; setbacks die away and shrivel with time. As I said before 'be careful who you call a salesperson' it is an accolade to be proud of! No matter what it is you sell or are thinking of selling, make sure you really believe in it. You can't sell something you believe to be second rate.

Salespeople operate on all kinds of different remuneration methods ranging from full commission through retainer and commission to salary and bonuses and on to straight salary. Whichever is your method, make sure it fits you. Make sure you are paid what you're worth! In other words, don't sell yourself short! If you feel you are of more value to your company, *say so.* You may be surprised at the response.

If you are running your own business, you already know how valuable your selling skills are to achieving success. Whether it is in selling your product or in handling a disgruntled customer. Your skills are worth gold!

Similarly if you are fortunate enough to employ a top salesperson, treat him or her properly. Don't take this person for granted.

I only say this because I have seen it happen so many times. A proprietor or sales manager has a minor confrontation with one of their top salespeople, pride intervenes and bingo a good person goes, and profits go down. Most top salespeople tend to be emotional. It's what they use to sell to people, to persuade clients to buy their product. It's a valuable asset!

On the other hand, the people who hold everything together; the accountants, managers, scientists and organisers tend to be logical thinkers and find salespeople difficult to understand. To these people I say, 'make an effort to understand your salespeople. It will pay dividends.'

To the salespeople I say, if you want to get something from the office, always remember you will, more than likely, be dealing with a logical thinker, and so adjust your approach accordingly. Use logical arguments.

Respect for everyone will always be the best way!

Now we have come to the end of this book on selling. Thank you for sticking with me!

But let me ask you to do two things, one for you and one for me.

First, one for you. *Start a journal.* Not just an ordinary journal, not a diary. No, this journal must be special. I would ask you, for your own sake to keep a journal of all the ideas you hear or see or read about, the ideas that touch *you*. *Write them down in your journal.* Review your journal regularly and you know what? One day an idea in your journal will take root in your mind *and grow!* It will have such an effect on you that your life will change and that idea will become yours. You never know it might just be the making of you!

The second thing I would like you to do is for me. If during the reading of this book you have found any of the concepts or ideas helpful, please drop me a line and let me know. My email address is below. Writing is a bit like talking in a vacuum, I know you are out there and I hope you have enjoyed what you have read. I would like to know.

HAPPY AND SUCCESSFUL SELLING!

Rick Mansfield.

rbmansfield@ozemail.com.au